The Waterford & Limerick Railway

by C.E.J. Fryer

THE OAKWOOD PRESS

© Oakwood Press 2000

British Library Cataloguing in Publication Data
A Record for this book is available from the British Library
ISBN 0 85361 543 8

Typeset by Oakwood Graphics.
Repro by Ford Graphics, Ringwood, Hants.
Printed by Oakdale Printing Co., Poole, Dorset.

Heading towards Limerick with a goods train on 17th June, 1954, class 'J15' 0-6-0 No. 161 bursts under the bridge at Athenry station. *A.C. Gilbert*

Title page: Locomotives Nos. 170 and 16 are seen arriving at Limerick with the 9.10 am from Sligo on 30th June, 1938. *H.C. Casserley*

Published by The Oakwood Press (Usk), P.O. Box 13, Usk, Mon., NP15 1YS.

E-Mail: oakwood-press@dial.pipex.com
Website: http://ds.dial.pipex.com/oakwood-press

Contents

Robinson 4-4-0 No. 298 (GSR class 'D15') is seen at Ennis on the 8th June, 1932 with the 8.55 am Sligo to Limerick train. *H.C. Casserley*

An early postcard view of Waterford station, with the city on the south bank of the River Suir connected to the station by the old toll bridge.   *Author's Collection*

The new roof on Limerick station in 1929, with class 'J11' 0-6-0T No. 217 handling the station pilot's duties.   *L&GRP*

Introduction

It was a common thing, in the age when railways were being built in the British Isles, for a small line, built to serve a local need with locally-raised money, to progress for a while independently but then to find it necessary to submit to the offers of a larger line and become absorbed into it, its shareholders exchanging their shares for shares in the larger concern. Business in the Victorian age matched the Darwinian concept of the survival of the fittest; financial and industrial nature, like that of the animal world, was red in tooth and claw and expected to be so. Where the Waterford & Limerick Railway (W&LR) differed from others was in the long-drawn-out period of its survival as an independent line, and its phenomenal growth, first working and then absorbing other lines, though its financial situation might have suggested corporate suicide on favourable terms long before this actually occurred.

However, as will be shown in a later chapter, there were forces operating which helped it to survive, and while this was so it kept up the illusion of a rise to greatness, and before the end of the 19th century it had become the fourth largest railway in Ireland, though the country's four largest cities were well outside its sphere of activity. Then the favouring influences ceased, and by 1899 it was clear that it could not carry on alone. After some protracted negotiations the largest railway in Ireland absorbed the fourth largest - and found the digestion difficult.

Material for a history of this interesting railway has not been easy to come by. The most helpful single source has been Bradshaw's *Shareholders' Guide*, in which annual reports from all the separate railways in Great Britain (which then included Ireland) were published for the benefit of people who wished to invest their money in railways and wanted to make an informed choice. In the reports from the W&LR one sees mirrored the growth of the line, its changing financial state, its working interests in other railways, and to some extent the disputes and disagreements within the ranks of its Directors and shareholders.

Unlike many other Irish railways constructed during the 19th century, the main line linking the two cities after which it was named is still in being, though all but two of its branches and extensions have ceased to carry passenger traffic and some have closed altogether. It is now more used for freight than for passenger trains. One can still, however, make the journey from Waterford to Limerick and back in a day all through the year - and twice a day during the summer - and find plenty of lineside interest. If fewer, the services are quicker than they were a century ago, and may well improve still more if the proposed railcars are introduced.

The line's period of glory was its final decade as an independent company. It had the good fortune to have then, as its locomotive, carriage and wagon superintendent one of the most famous of British locomotive engineers in the days of steam, J.G. Robinson, who learned and developed at Limerick the skills and expertise that were subsequently to make him famous on the Great Central. He gave his engines and carriages the most colourful livery then to be seen in Ireland, and the outlines of the few locomotives he designed at Limerick foreshadow the graceful aspects of those he later built for the Great Central Railway. It is a pity that he predated the time of colour photography and the days when talented painters exercised their abilities in making portraits of engines and trains. Cuthbert Hamilton Ellis would have been just the man to perpetuate a Robinson 2-4-0 or 4-4-0 in paint, hauling one of the boat trains against a background of an

Irish landscape, with two children in late Victorian costume looking on admiringly. Alas, there is a shortage even of black-and-white photographs from the 1890s, and nobody thought to describe it verbally at the time either. There are one or two magazine articles and that is all. But the line is still well worth a visit, both for its own sake and for the attractive surroundings, the lush countryside and the charming Irish towns where one can stroll around and imagine oneself being there 50 years ago, for they have not changed much since then. It is still a long way to Tipperary, but the trip is still worth making.

Chapter One

Early Unfulfilled Proposals

As in England, so in Ireland the first proposal for a public railway to convey both passengers and goods was not, as might have been expected, for a line to serve the country's principal city, Dublin, but for one to connect two large provincial centres. In this it resembled the Liverpool & Manchester Railway (L&MR), which issued its first Prospectus in 1824, and the Parliamentary Bill for which became an Act in the same month in 1826 as the Act which authorised the Irish line, the Limerick & Waterford Railway (which was the title originally proposed).

The two undertakings differed considerably. The English railway was to be a little over 30 miles long, and would link two of the largest urban centres in Europe; the Limerick & Waterford line was to be more than twice that length, and the places it was to connect were much smaller. Whereas the English line connected a large manufacturing city with its nearest port, the Irish railway was to link two ports. The L&MR could not expect much custom from intermediate places; it was expected that the Limerick & Waterford *would* do so as its route was to pass through one of the most productive regions of Ireland and would take in quite a few sizeable towns *en route*. While the intention of the promoters of the L&MR was from the first to carry not only goods but passengers, the Parliamentary Act which sanctioned the construction of the Irish line nowhere makes mention of the latter, though it is evident from Alexander Nimmo's commentary, cited later in this chapter, that passenger transport was also envisaged. Finally, while the English railway was soon built and working, the Irish one never got under way and the powers it had been given eventually lapsed. Not until 20 years later was the scheme revived.

The Act that first authorised the construction of a line from Limerick in the direction of Waterford came into effect on 31st May, 1826. Its intention, stated ponderously and at length in its opening section, was as follows:

Whereas the making and maintaining of a Railway or Railways, Tramroad or Tramroads, together with the three several Branches therefrom herein-after mentioned, with proper Works and Conveniences adjoining thereto or connected therewith, for the Passage of Waggons, Carts and other Carriages properly constructed, commencing at or near to the End of the Canal Lock in *Clare Street* in the Parish of *Saint Patrick* in the City of Limerick, and passing from thence through the several Parishes or Places hereinafter mentioned, to and terminating at or near to a certain place called or known by the Name of the *Osier Beds* at the town of *Carrick** in the Parish of *Saint Nicholas* in the Barony of *Iffa* and *Offa East* in the *County of Tipperary*, would be of great Advantage to the Inhabitants of the said Counties, Towns or Places, by forming a direct Communication between the Rivers *Suir* and *Shannon*, and by opening an expeditious and cheap Communication between the agricultural and mineral Counties of *Limerick, Tipperary, Kilkenny* and *Waterford*, and the great commercial Cities of *Limerick* and *Waterford*, and the other large and populous Towns on the line of such Railway or Tramroad, and by

---

* Carrick on Suir; here the promoters presumed in the first instance that goods would be unloaded on to barges, or loaded from them; Waterford itself would be reached later on by an extension of the line, for which another Act would be needed.

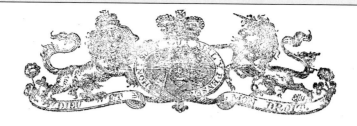

ANNO SEPTIMO

GEORGII IV. REGIS.

✱✱✱

Cap. cxxxix.

An Act for making and maintaining a Railway or Tramroad from the City of *Limerick* to the Town of *Carrick* in the County of *Tipperary*, with several Branches therefrom in the County of *Tipperary* aforesaid and in the County of the City of *Waterford*.   [31st *May* 1826.]

WHEREAS the making and maintaining of a Railway or Railways, Tramroad or Tramroads, together with the Three several Branches therefrom herein-after mentioned, with proper Works and Conveniences adjoining thereto or connected therewith, for the Passage of Waggons, Carts, and other Carriages properly constructed, commencing at or near to the End of the Canal Lock in *Clare Street* in the Parish of *Saint Patrick* in the City of *Limerick*, and passing from thence, through the several Parishes or Places herein-after mentioned, to and terminating at or near to a certain Place called or known by the Name of the *Osier Beds* at the Town of *Carrick* in the Parish of *Saint Nicholas* in the Barony of *Iffa* and *Offa East* in the County of *Tipperary* aforesaid, would be of great Advantage to the Inhabitants of the said Counties, Towns, or Places, by forming a direct Communication between the Rivers *Suir* and *Shannon*, and by opening an expeditious and cheap Communication between the agricultural and mineral Counties of *Limerick*, *Tipperary*, *Kilkenny*, and *Waterford*, and the great commercial Cities of *Limerick* and *Waterford*, and the other large and populous Towns on the Line of such

[*Local.*]   45 *F*   Railway

Part of the beginning of the 1826 Act of Parliament authorising the building of a railway between Limerick and Carrick-on-Suir.   *By courtesy of the Librarian, House of Lords, London*

affording an additional Mode of Transit for Merchandize and other Articles between those Places, and also to and from the neighbouring Country, would be of great public Utility: And whereas the several Persons herein-after named are willing and desirous, at their own Expence, to make and maintain the said Railways or Tramroads and collateral Branches; but the same cannot be effected without the Aid and Authority of Parliament: May it therefore please Your Majesty that it may be enacted; and be it enacted by the King's Most Excellent Majesty by and with the Advice and Consent of the Lords Spiritual and Temporal and Commons, in this present Parliament assembled, and by the Authority of the same, That the Right Honourable the *Earl of Belfast*, *Thomas Haviland Burke*, *Henry Houldsworth Hunt*, *John Easthope*, *James Hubbersly*, *Richard Davis*, *Henry Sarjent*, *J. Flather*, *James Charles Michell*, *Robert Walters*, *Henry Egerton*, *John William Bannister*, *John Crafts*, *John Fraser*, *Michael Colesworthy*, *John Moss*, *Charles Williams Allen*, *Gordon*, *Cuerton*, *Forster*, *King*,* and all and every other Person and Persons, Body and Bodies Politic and Corporate, who shall hereafter become Subscribers to the Undertaking, and their several and respective Successors, Executors, Administrators and Assigns, shall be and they are hereby united into a Company for making completing and maintaining the said Railway or Railways, or Tramroad or Tramroads, and Branches, and other Works by this Act authorized to be made and executed according to the Rules, Orders and Directions herein-after mentioned, and for that Purpose shall be one Body Corporate, by the Name and Style of 'The *Limerick* and *Waterford* Railway Company', and by that Name shall have perpetual Succession, and shall have a Common Seal, and by that Name shall and may sue and be sued; and the said Company shall have Power and Authority, from and after the passing of this Act, and at all Times thereafter, to purchase and hold Lands and Hereditaments to them and their Successors and Assigns for the use of the said Undertaking and Works, and also to sell and dispose of the said Lands and Hereditaments again in manner by this Act directed, without incurring any of the Penalties and Forfeitures of the Statutes of Mortmain.

The Act itself is immensely lengthy, some 40,000 words in all. Its size reflects the fact that no General Acts of Parliament had yet been passed for the regulation of all railways in the United Kingdom, so that in this particular enactment all conceivable situations had to be provided for, major or minor. For example, Section 5 reads:

And be it further enacted, That every Steam Engine which shall be erected by the said Company in pursuance of this Act shall be constructed upon the best and most approved Principle of consuming the Smoke arising therefrom.

Similarly, Section 97 dealt with the possibility of lunatics and minors voting at the company's meetings, and who might exercise this right in their stead.

Sadly, this enormous document, which must have occupied many hours of clerkly labour, was in the end all to no purpose. No rails were ever laid, no locomotives travelling on them consumed their own smoke, no lunatics or minors ever affected the company's fortunes through votes cast by their representatives. Money was not forthcoming to pay for the line and local opposition arose to its construction. Nevertheless it had strong supporters. One is fortunate to have discovered, in the Public Library in Limerick, a Report by the engineer Alexander Nimmo who, writing when construction was still a possibility, put forward his own comments, along with a detailed survey to which he in places alludes. He thought that the line, once it had been made,

---

* The forenames of the last four persons mentioned were not included but spaces were left for their insertion.

would be able to pay for itself. In regard to this he is very persuasive, and perhaps over-confident. He prefaced his Report with

> . . . a few observations on the general nature of the undertaking and the description and probable amount of the business that may be expected. The object is to establish a more direct, cheap and expeditious communication than now exists across the south of Ireland, and through that highly-productive part of it which has emphatically been named The Golden Vale; to lower the rate of transporting its numerous productions to the seaport towns; to facilitate the supplies of fuel and imported articles; and especially to take advantage of the establishment of steam packets across the Channel [i.e. St George's Channel between south east Ireland and Pembrokeshire] for sending its produce with despatch and certainty into the English markets. For this purpose it is proposed to lay an iron railway between the cities of Limerick and Waterford by the towns of Tipperary, Cahir, Clonmel and Carrick, and to run branches into the main line from other places of importance.

Nimmo prefaces his account with some general remarks about the methods of conveying goods on a railway, and looks forward to its wide development:

> Railways as hitherto constructed have been chiefly used to convey articles of great weight and small value in situations where canal navigation was impracticable, or where the temporary nature of the traffic would not pay the expenses of one. The trade being chiefly in one direction, they have been usually made with a gentle declivity, following, like canals, the contour of the rising grounds . . . Where great declivities occur, the loaded carriage is attached to a rope or chain passing round a pully at top, and by its descent elevates an empty one, the motion of the carriage being regulated by a brake wheel.
>
> This is called a self-acting plane, and by late experiments it is found applicable to slopes so gentle as one foot in thirty feet, and thus a considerable horizontal motion is obtained at little expence. When necessary to elevate the loaded carriage, it was done by a fixed winding engine at the top of the plane, impelled by water-wheels, horses or steam, in minor cases by the ordinary crab windlass wrought by men.
>
> Railways of this description have been hitherto in a great measure confined to the vicinity of mines or manufactories, or great public works, and in a few instances they have been thought applicable to the conveyance of goods or passengers. But some late improvements have opened a new view of the matter, and it now appears probable that railways will be soon adopted on all great thoroughfares for the sake of expedition, as well as for their cheapness beyond every other species of carriage.

He goes on to insist on the necessity of easy grading, which may make excavation and embankment obligatory, particularly with lines which did not depend (as so many colliery-to-riverside railways did) on gravity for the movement of goods in one direction only. The course of the line he was recommending was generally the same as the one later adopted and which was specified in the Act of 1826. He envisages the use of horse traction, and also the employment of 'locomotive engines' which will have the advantage of speed. The rails themselves, he recommends, should consist of 'flat bars of merchantable iron . . . rolled thicker at the top, as well for additional strength as to lessen the wear of wheels, and to enable them, if any pilferage be attempted, to be more readily identified'. (One may smile at the notion of thieves unscrewing rails and taking them away, but as they would then be made only a couple of yards or so long this would have been perfectly possible.) He also suggests 'a continuous bearing or curb or stone below the rails throughout'.

As to the waggons, he suggests that the wheels should have flat rims about three inches broad, with a central groove to fit over the rail edges; thus the vehicles would be able to travel on roads when this was necessary. He expects little friction in bearings because

> . . . in practice we find the friction of the railways to be so small that when the fall exceeds one inch in a perch, or 1 in 252, the waggons begin to follow the horses with little or no effort on straight roads. The edge railways in use in the north of England seem by various experiments to have a friction from $\frac{1}{70}$th to $\frac{1}{80}$th of the weight; we may therefore safely consider the friction on good railways as not more than $\frac{1}{150}$th part of the load.

He emphasises how much easier it will be for a horse to pull a load along a railway.

> The power of draft which a horse exerts on a road or railway is found to be about 150 lbs. when he goes at the rate of two miles per hour. With such a railway as those above-mentioned, where the force required to overcome friction is the one-hundred-and-fiftieth part of the weight, such a horse would draw 22,500 lbs, or above 10 tons, including the carriages. It is well known that on the best of our common roads the load of a horse never exceeds 1½ tons, or about 22 times the power, so that by a railway the expence of horse power would be reduced to the one-sixth of what is necessary on the best roads.
>
> On a canal a horse would draw double the weight at the same rate of two miles per hour, but the proportion in greater velocities speedily turns in favour of the railway, on account of the rapidly-increasing resistance of the water . . .
>
> The superiority of the railway over the canal will be still more manifest if we attempt greater velocities, for at nine miles an hour, the horse being supposed to exert only nine pounds in traction, he will draw 1,350 lbs. on the railway. Such a velocity on a canal may be considered altogether unattainable.

He goes on to consider the further advantages of the application of steam, whether to operate a winding engine that pulls loads on a rope, or a locomotive. If steam traction is used, then he suggests that turf (i.e. peat), locally obtainable from Irish bogs in great quantities, would be the most economical form of fuel.

He then proceeds to estimate the potential profitably of the line, should it be constructed. What trade, whether in imports, exports or in local carriage of goods, might it be expected to attract, and what revenue might accrue in consequence? Beginning with a description of the nature of the country through which the railway would pass, and the existing mining and excavation activities in turf, low-grade coal, limestone for producing lime to improve soil fertility, and building stone, he goes on to consider the local industries and the populations of the towns and districts who could benefit from the railway bringing supplies of food or other materials. Comparing the proposed railway with the existing Grand Canal that linked Dublin with the Shannon, he calculates that with similar charges the railway would attract business from the regions which the canal could not serve - more particularly in the carriage of turf, limestone, slates, corn and potatoes. (The latter was a necessary staple food for the poorer Irish, as the distress and starvation caused by the subsequent potato famine of 1845-1849 demonstrated.) One commodity he mentions as likely to produce as much revenue as the carriage of potatoes is 'the return of manure from the towns' to the countryside for fertilising the land - an item that would not spring to mind at the present time as meriting extensive carriage by rail!

His only comments on possible passenger traffic, in foreseeing the extent of which he could have had no guidance, were incidental to the movement of goods, and read rather amusingly:

> The supply of the various market towns with milk, butter, hay and straw will be highly worthy of attention, and will be greatly promoted, as also the transit of passengers, by having light caravans running at a quick rate at stated hours on the railroad.

Reckoning only on the country which depended on Waterford for imports and exports, he estimated that, in internal traffic, 3½ million ton-miles of carriage would be attracted to the railway, 2 million ton-miles in goods for export and almost one million in imports. All this, he reckoned, would produce a total revenue of just over £40,000 annually. These estimates, he believed, were conservative ones.

Nimmo's optimism was evidently not shared by others, since the promotion of the line ran up against opposition from local landowning interests, and there was a reluctance to buy shares. For some 10 years the project hung fire. Meanwhile a Royal Commission was appointed to inquire into the manner in which railway communication could be most advantageously promoted in Ireland, and this body issued its report in 1837. It recommended the making of a main trunk line from Dublin to Cork and a lateral line from Limerick to Waterford, the two crossing about four miles from Cahir. This differed from the pattern that materialised later, when the line to Cork was routed north of the Galtee mountains instead of south of them, so that the crossing came further to the north-west, beyond Tipperary. No action, however, was taken immediately; it was not until 1845 that another Act of Parliament was passed authorising the building of the Waterford & Limerick Railway, to which the next chapter alludes.

Chapter Two

The Parliamentary Acts of 1845 and 1847

The second Act of Parliament authorising the construction of a railway between Limerick and Waterford received the Royal Assent on 21st July, 1845. This time the initiative had come from the latter city; it is the first named in the proposed title and the specified route begins there. The Act itself was very much shorter than the previous one had been, since many pieces of legislation regulating the building of railways in the United Kingdom had now come into effect, and it was only necessary to specify that they applied to the railway now proposed. The Preamble of the Act declares:

> Whereas the making of a Railway from the Borough or City of *Waterford* to the Borough or City of *Limerick*, with a Branch diverging therefrom, would be of great public Advantage, by opening an additional, certain and expeditious Means of Communication between the said Places, and also by facilitating Communication between more distant Towns and Places: And whereas the Persons hereafter named are willing, at their own Expence, to carry such an undertaking into Execution, but the same cannot be effected without the Authority of Parliament: May it therefore please Your Majesty that it may be enacted, and be it enacted by the Queen's Most Excellent Majesty, by and with the Advice and Consent of the Lords Spiritual and Temporal, and Commons, in this present Parliament assembled, and by the Authority of the same, That the said several Acts of Parliament following, (that is to say) the 'Companies Clauses Consolidation Act, 1845', the 'Lands Clauses Consolidation Act, 1845', and the 'Railway Clauses Consolidation Act, 1845', shall be incorporated with and form Part of this Act.

Fifty-seven persons are named as Subscribers, as compared with only 21 in the 1826 Act, and no person's name appears in both Acts - which is perhaps not surprising after a lapse of almost 20 years. The estimated cost of building the line was more than double the previous estimate - £750,000 against £324,225. Fifteen thousand shares of £50 each were to provide the capital, and there might be additional borrowing of up to £250,000. Twelve persons are named as the original Directors, all but one being chosen from among the sponsors. The route specified was more or less the same as that proposed earlier, and is spelt out at length in a single enormous sentence over 1,200 words long.

The place of origin of the line is stated as

> . . . the Right or South Bank of the River Suir at or near certain Premises called The Waterford Coal Company's Yard, in the Townland of Newtown in the Parish of St John's Without, in the Borough or City of Waterford.

It was to run south of the Suir as far as Killoteran, and then cross the river and make northwards to Ballincurra, where it reached the route of the present line and went on to pass the town of Carrick-on-Suir to the south. West of Carrick it kept near the north bank of the Suir; then, four miles short of Clonmel, it crossed the river and continued along the south bank, diverging from the actual course taken later and going well south of Clonmel. Crossing the Suir again two miles

ANNO OCTAVO & NONO

VICTORIÆ REGINÆ.

❧✶✶✶

Cap. cxxxi.

An Act for making and maintaining a Railway from the City of *Waterford* to the City of *Limerick*, with Branches. [21st *July* 1845.]

WHEREAS the making of a Railway from the Borough or City of *Waterford* to the Borough or City of *Limerick*, with a Branch diverging therefrom, would be of great public Advantage, by opening an additional, certain, and expeditious Means of Communication between the said Places, and also by facilitating Communication between more distant Towns and Places : And whereas the Persons hereafter named are willing, at their own Expence, to carry such Undertaking into execution, but the same cannot be effected without the Authority of Parliament : May it therefore please Your Majesty that it may be enacted ; and be it enacted by the Queen's most Excellent Majesty, by and with the Advice and Consent of the Lords Spiritual and Temporal, and Commons, in this present Parliament assembled, and by the Authority of the same, That the said several Acts of Parliament following, (that is to say,) the " Companies Clauses Consolidation Act, 1845," the " Lands Clauses Consolidation Act, 1845," and the " Railway Clauses Consolidation Act, 1845," shall be incorporated with and form Part of this Act.

Incorporation of 8 & 9 Vict. cc. 16. 18. and 20. with this Act.

II. And be it enacted, That in citing this Act in other Acts of Parliament, and in legal Instruments, it shall be sufficient to use the Expression

Short Title.

[*Local.*] 31 *E*

Part of the beginning of the 1845 Act of Parliament authorising the building of the Waterford & Limerick Railway. *By courtesy of the Librarian, House of Lords, London*

further on, it rejoined the present route and continued westwards until, two miles south of Cahir, it turned towards that town, crossed the Suir for the last time, curved around the eastern end of the Galtee More range and left the Suir valley, cut across the entrance to the Glen of Aherlow and passed just to the south of Tipperary on a rising gradient. Going northwards, it crossed the projected route of the Great Southern & Western Railway (GS&WR) about 106 miles from Dublin, with which it was later to make a link with a spur line so that the GS&WR would have a route to Limerick with running powers. The planned route now became that of the existing line all the way to Limerick, where it terminated 'at or near the East Side of Nelson Street in the Townland of Priorsland'.

The Act specified the tolls that had to be paid by users of the railway; this section makes interesting reading.

XXXIV. And be it enacted, That it shall not be lawful for the said Company to charge in respect of the several Articles, Matters and Things, and of the several Descriptions of Animals herein-after mentioned, conveyed on the Railway by this Act authorized, any greater Sum, including the Charges for the Use of Carriages, Waggons or Trucks, and for Locomotive Power, and all other Charges incidental to such Conveyance (except a reasonable Charge for the Expence of loading and unloading where such Service is performed by the Company), than the several Sums here-after mentioned; (that is to say,) For all Dung, Compost, and all sorts of Manure, Lime and Limestone, and all undressed Materials for the Repair of public Roads or Highways, and for all Coals, per Ton per Mile, one Penny Halfpenny;

For all Coke, Culm,* Charcoal and Cinders, all Stones for Building, Pitching and Paving, all Bricks, Tiles, Slates, Clay, Sand, Ironstone and Iron Ore, Pig Iron, Bar Iron, Rod Iron, Hoop Iron, and all other similar Descriptions of Wrought Iron and Iron Castings not manufactured into Utensils or other Articles of Merchandize, per Ton per Mile, Two Pence.

For all Sugar, Grain, Corn, Flour, Hides, Dyewoods, Earthenware, Timber, Staves and Deals, Metals (except Iron,) Nails, Anvils, Vices and Chains, per Ton per Mile, Three Pence;

For all Cotton and other Wools, Drugs, manufactured Goods, and all other Wares, Merchandise, Fish, Articles, Matters or Things, per Ton per Mile Four Pence;

And for every Carriage, of whatever Description, and not being a Carriage adapted and used for travelling on a Railway, per Mile Seven Pence;

For every Horse, Mule, Ass, or other Beast of Draught or Burden, per Mile, Five Pence;

For every Ox, Cow, Bull or Neat Cattle, per Mile, Two Pence;

For every Calf or Pig, one Mile one Penny

For every Sheep, Lamb or other small Animal, per Mile Three Farthings.

XXXV. And be it enacted, That it shall not be lawful for the said Company to demand and receive any greater Sum in respect of the Carriage of Passengers conveyed on the Railway by this Act authorized than Three Pence per Passenger per Mile in respect to any Passenger travelling in a First-class Carriage, Two Pence per Passenger per Mile in respect of any Passenger travelling in a Second-class Carriage, and One Penny per Passenger per Mile in respect of any Passenger travelling in a Third-class Carriage, including the Charges for the Use of Carriages and Locomotive Power, and all other Charges incidental to such Conveyance, unless in the Case of Passengers travelling by Special Trains.

In regard to 'Small Packages and single Articles of great Weight', the company was allowed to make such charges as it thought fit. Passengers' Luggage Allowances were not as generous as they were later to be; a first class passenger might take 100 lb., a second class passenger 60 lb., and a third class passenger 40 lb. free of charge.

* A poor-quality type of coal, mined locally.

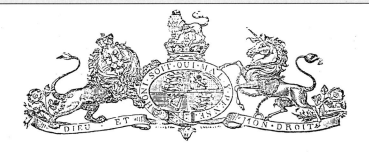

ANNO DECIMO & UNDECIMO

VICTORIÆ REGINÆ.

****

Cap. ccxxxi.

An Act to authorize certain Alterations in the Line of the *Waterford and Limerick* Railway, and to amend the Act relating thereto; and for other Purposes. **[22d *July* 1847.]**

WHEREAS an Act was passed in the Eighth and Ninth Years of the Reign of Her present Majesty, intituled *An Act* **8 & 9 Vict.** *for making and maintaining a Railway from the City of* **c. 131.** Waterford *to the City of* Limerick, *with Branches:* And whereas it is expedient that certain Portions of the Line of the *Waterford and Limerick* Railway as authorized to be made by the said recited Act should be abandoned, and the new or altered Lines of Railway hereinafter particularly described should be made in lieu thereof: And whereas the *Waterford and Limerick* Railway Company are desirous of carrying into effect the Objects aforesaid, if authorized by Parliament so to do; but for such Purpose it is necessary that some of the Powers and Provisions of the said recited Act should be enlarged, and further Powers granted to the said Company: May it therefore please Your Majesty that it may be enacted; and be it enacted by the Queen's most Excellent Majesty, by and with the Advice and Consent of the Lords Spiritual and Temporal, and Commons, in this present Parliament assembled, and by the Authority of the same, **8 & 9 Vict.** That the Provisions of the "Lands Clauses Consolidation Act, 1845," **cc. 18. & 20. extended to**

[*Local.*   36 *S*   **and this Act.**

The Act provided for the joint use of the line by the owning company and the Great Southern & Western Railway from the point where the Waterford-Limerick and Dublin-Cork routes crossed. The latter line was to have running powers between that point and Limerick, though it was envisaged that it would have a separate station there from that of the former line. The W&LR undertook to have this part of the line finished no later than the completion of the GS&WR line to Cork, and the two companies were to agree on what rent the GS&WR should pay for using it. Separate accounts were to be kept for this section of line.

As the work of constructing the line progressed, changes were found to be necessary and further Parliamentary authorisation was required, so that a fresh Bill was presented to Parliament, which became an Act on 22nd July, 1847, the preamble stating:

> Whereas an Act was passed in the Eighth and Ninth years of Her Present Majesty, intituled An Act for making and maintaining a Railway from the City of *Waterford* to the City of *Limerick,* with Branches; And whereas it is expedient that certain Portions of the Line of the *Waterford and Limerick Railway* as authorized to be made by the said recited Act should be abandoned, and the new or altered Lines of Railway herein-after particularly described should be made in lieu thereof; And whereas the *Waterford and Limerick Railway Company* are desirous of carrying into effect the Objects aforesaid, if authorized by Parliament to do so; but for such Purpose it is necessary that some of the Powers and Provisions of the said recited Act should be enlarged, and further Powers granted to the said Company: May it therefore please Your Majesty (&c., &c.)

The alterations applied to two sections between Clonmel and Cahir and one north of Tipperary, where deviations had become necessary from the route as marked on the original plans. The third seems to have resulted from objections made by a local landowner, one Hugh Baker Esq., since later in the Act it specifies that the deviated line should not go nearer to the entrance of the avenue which led to his house than 118 yards, and that a wall six feet high and two feet thick should be built on the east side of the line at this place, presumably to hide it from his sensitive eyes and ears.

The Act further extended by two more years the period during which lands might be taken for the line's construction, so that the deviations could be completed. Various other sections within it dealt with minor matters regarding share-forfeiture, the issue of new shares and the payment of dividends. Section 21 is of interest in showing that some of the work involved in building the line was performed by local peasantry under the provisions of a previous Act, 'to facilitate the Employment of the labouring Poor for a limited Period in the distressed Districts of Ireland'. Payment for such work done for the company was authorized to be made to the proper authorities. At the time when the line was being built there was great distress throughout rural Ireland because of the repeated failure of the potato crop through a blight. Potatoes were the poor Irishman's staple food, and because of this disaster millions starved to death or emigrated. The above-mentioned Act was in effect a means of giving public aid to mitigate the effects of the famine - but the 'labouring Poor' were required to labour for their subsistence; there were no free hand-outs, even to the starving.

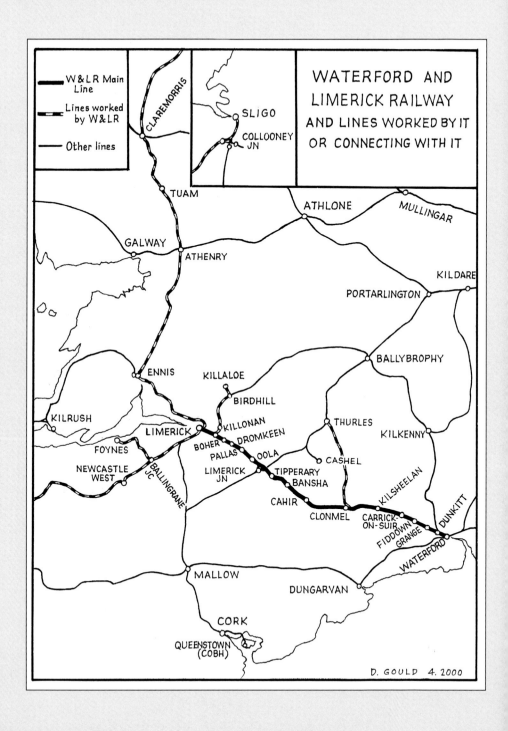

Chapter Three

Constructing the Line

The work of surveying the proposed railway between Waterford & Limerick had been entrusted to Charles Vignoles, an Irishman who, after a period of service in the British Army, became a civil engineer and was involved in the planning and construction of many railways in the United Kingdom before going abroad to do the same in places as far afield as Russia and Brazil. The project to build a line in his own native country between two of its chief ports engaged his particular interest from 1841 onwards, and when the Waterford & Limerick company was formed in 1844 he was appointed as its Chief Engineer. He supported the company vigorously when its Bill was opposed in Parliament by another company, the proposed Dublin & Cashel Railway, on the grounds that the W&LR could serve the needs of the area between Tipperary and Limerick better than the Dublin company, and was able to engage the support of Sir Robert Peel who was then Prime Minister.

Once Parliamentary sanction had been obtained the building of the line began. There was good reason for this to commence at Limerick rather than Waterford. The construction of the Great Southern & Western Railway had already started, and its designated route crossed that of the W&LR some 22 miles from Limerick, so that traffic between the latter city and the capital might be expected as soon as the two lines reached the point of intersection. This actually occurred at the beginning of July 1848, when a junction was made between the two railways. The moment was signalised by a ceremonial opening by the GS&WR of a through route between the two cities, which took place at the Junction and was attended by many prominent figures in Irish society. The occasion was not entirely a happy one, for there was widespread discontent throughout the country at this time against the British Government and its representatives. According to the *Freeman's Journal*, which supported the anti-English cause, a crowd of workmen at the Junction, who had each been given a shilling to applaud the Viceroy after he had made a speech, instead produced the equivalent of a slow hand-clap, 'one of the most consumptive cheers we ever heard'.

This was two months after the line from Limerick had been completed as far as Tipperary. The W&LR project had been set in hand, despite the fact that money was short, largely because the contractor had been obliging enough to take shares in the line in lieu of much of the payment due to him. At the beginning of 1846 only £85,000 had been contributed, but this was reckoned to be sufficient to reach Tipperary, three miles beyond the crossing point with the mooted route of the GS&WR. Cargo-loads of materials carried in coastwise steamers reached Limerick by sea; meanwhile the purchase of land was arranged between Limerick and Tipperary, and the terminal station at Limerick was built. Local labour was used, and an eminent Irish engineer, Richard Osborne, who successfully master-minded the construction of the Philadelphia and Reading Railroad in the USA, was appointed by Vignoles to be resident

Engineer. The contract for building the line was given to William Dargan, the constructor of several other Irish railways, who after the extension of the GS&WR from Thurles to Cork had been sanctioned received the contract for that as well.

The first 25 miles from Limerick to Tipperary went ahead quite quickly, there being no natural obstacles of any consequence to be removed by excavation or bridging, and the line reached the village of Pallas, a little over half-way, by mid-June 1947. Such difficulties as there were came not from the terrain but from obstructive landlords and dissatisfied workmen. As an example of the first: a certain Samuel Dickson, of George Street, Limerick, demanded compensation from the company for injury to four properties which he possessed, 'by severance or otherwise from construction from such portion of the railway as will pass through the same'. The company made him an offer which he rejected as insufficient. The dispute then went to court, and Dickson was awarded a sum less than the company had originally offered him; in addition he was required to pay the legal costs, which must have used up a large part of the £279 which he was allotted as compensation. His feelings may be imagined.

Another court case dealt with a different kind of grievance. During the 19th century the 'Combination Laws' were still in force, preventing workmen from forming unions to protect or secure the right to receive adequate wages and satisfactory working conditions. To attempt to organise a 'combination' for such a purpose was a breach of these laws, which might result in the penalty of transportation to Australia, where some penal settlements still existed - as had happened in the case of the 'Tolpuddle Martyrs' in 1834. Court records at Limerick in February 1846 include the following:

> Mr Geoghan, Superintendent of the Waterford and Limerick Railway Works at the terminus near the city charged John Cavanagh, a labourer, with instigating the workmen to turn out for advance of wages and inducement to leave their employment. The charge was fully sustained by evidence, and Alderman Watson, as Chairman of the Bench, said he regretted that at the present moment, when wages and employment are so generally complained of, a body of men should be so unmindful of their families as to commit such illegal and wanton conduct as to deprive them of their means of support. It was also to be lamented that the Railway Company should be put to such trouble. Those same people were so glad to seek employment from the Railway and receive an amount of wages they scarcely contemplated twelve months since. The Magistrates did not intend to deal summarily with the case, which was subject officially to transportation. The case was sent before a higher tribunal.

One hopes the poor man and his supporters were not transported. The pay they were actually receiving was nine shillings a week. Whether or not Mr Cavanagh's action was morally reprehensible, let others judge, but it was probably inadvisable, since Ireland was then in a more distressed state than ever before or since. The famine which followed the blight on the potato crop was then reaching its height, so that hundreds of thousands of poor Irishmen were desperately seeking for work. Cavanagh was trying to sell his and his companions' labour in a buyer's market.

At about this time Richard Osborne was employing between 150 and 200 men per mile, choosing them from the enormous numbers which flocked from all parts of Ireland to get work if they could - and in many cases died from hunger if they could not. The work was not without its risks. On 15th June, 1847 the *Limerick Recorder* reported a fatal accident.

As the workmen were taking away from a pit the trunking stuff for the Limerick-Tipperary Railway, the upper part of a bank fell in and, striking on the breast of a labourer of the name of Hall, threw him backwards on a great stone which lay behind. From this situation he was immediately raised by his fellow-labourers in a state of insensibility, but as there had fallen on him only a small quantity of earth some hopes of life were entertained, and accordingly every means of resuscitation then at hand were resorted to. The Reverend J. Murphy, who had been at the time in discharge of his priestly duties nearby, came immediately to the spot and gave his valuable assistance, but the poor man was dead. As the corpse was borne from the fatal spot along the railway towards New Pallas, the heart-rending cries and lamentations of his widow and four children visibly affected the spectators. From his care and labours Hall's poor family expected protection and food, but with him these hopes are gone for ever.

On 9th May, 1848 the railway reached Tipperary and was opened to the public that far, with three intermediate stations, at Killonan, Pallas and Oola. Announcing the provision of a special train to make the journey, the *Limerick Chronicle* quoted fares of 4s. 6d. first class, 3s. second class and 1s. 8d. third class for the whole journey which was to take an hour and a half. At an average speed of 17 miles an hour, including the three stops, the train would not need to exceed 25 mph anywhere, and this was probably just as well since such things as continuous braking were still not known. A week and a half later the *Chronicle* offered its congratulations and approval to the company.

The line of rail between this City and Tipperary, we are rejoiced to perceive, is daily thronged with passengers and traffic luggage. It is sincerely hoped the undertaking may afford that benefit to the shareholders which they deservedly merit, as through their directors they have evinced an anxious disposition to afford the public every facility and accommodation. Travellers by this line enjoy the comfort of superior and elegantly fitted out second class carriages, an example which should be followed by the directors of the GS&W Railway, as passengers conveyed by the latter loudly complain of the rough and uncomfortable second class vehicles.

It was a short way to Tipperary; Waterford, however, was still far distant, and money had by now run out. There was a protracted delay before construction could be continued. Preference stock was issued and the Government was approached for help. The latter was now well aware of its responsibilities to relieve distress in Ireland, for the potato famine had caused deaths by the million, and something like a national conscience had been aroused. The Public Works Loan Commissioners made a grant of £120,000, and this permitted a start to be made south-eastwards from Tipperary in 1851, though there was a change from the original intention in that the line was made single instead of double track. Clonmel was reached in April of the following year, Fiddown a year after that. In August 1853 Dunkitt was reached, and served for a year as the terminus for Waterford, until a year later, a station was established a little short of half a mile from Waterford itself, on the north side of the Suir, the town itself being on the south side. It was to be a further eight years before the railhead was moved on to the present site of Waterford station, more conveniently situated close to the north end of the main bridge across the river into Waterford itself. The first train to run the whole distance from Limerick made the journey on 12th September, 1854, to the accompaniment of much rejoicing and flag-waving at either end. Ireland's first cross-country railway route was now open, and expectant eyes looked across St George's Channel to the port of New Milford, whence traffic from England was now expected since the South Wales Railway, later to be a part of the Great Western system, was approaching completion, and the shortest possible railway-and-sea route between Southern England and Southern Ireland would soon be an accomplished fact.

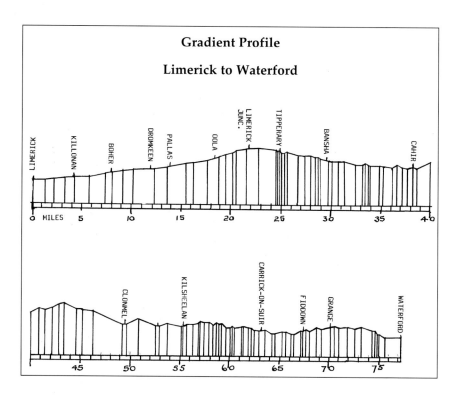

Chapter Four

The Management of the Line
1848-1900

As an independent concern, with its own Directors, shareholders and subordinate officials, the Waterford & Limerick Railway lasted for 53½ years, during just over 46 of which it actually linked the places after which it was named. It was never very strong financially, and existed uneasily in the shadow of two other companies, one English, the other Irish. Nevertheless it possessed a large appetite, absorbing other railways by agreement at intervals after spending some years working them. In its last few years it was, by Irish standards, a very large railway system, including several branches and a continuous line which extended almost to Sligo from Waterford, a distance nearly as far as from London to Plymouth. Eventually it could no longer exist on its own, and was absorbed by its larger neighbour, the Great Southern & Western. This chapter deals with its management during the half-century of its independent existence, the story of which can be largely pieced together from the yearly reports of its progress which appeared in successive volumes of Bradshaw's *Shareholders' Guide*.

The Board of Directors, formed mostly by persons of prominence resident in the area which the line was to serve, more particularly around Waterford, numbered at different times between nine and fifteen. At first, for some years, it was chaired by the Earl of Glengall; then, after two short tenures of the post by Major Massey of Tipperary and John Connolly of Dublin, it was occupied for 12 years by an important local figure in Waterford who owned a shipping company, William Malcomson, a strong-minded person who laid down the law to the company's employees and managed by his influence to keep the concern reasonably prosperous. He retired from the Chairmanship in 1872, in circumstances related below, and his Deputy Chairman, Abraham Stephens, succeeded him for three years during what proved to be a very troublesome period. Stephens was the longest-serving Board member, being a Director continuously from 1860 to 1890, during which period he was five years the Chairman and twelve the Vice Chairman. Other later prominent Chairmen were Thomas Synnott of Dublin, Sir James Spaight of Limerick and Percival Bernard of Tuam.

One English railway was actively concerned in the affairs and fortunes of the W&LR, the Great Western Railway of England, and the first Secretary of the Irish line was probably selected because of his family connection with his namesake in the same position on the GWR; this was William Saunders.* A glance at a map of the British Isles will explain the two railways' mutual concern. The GWR was then reaching out into South Wales, and as early as 1854 Bradshaw's *Guide* speaks of 'a broad-gauge competition for the Dublin traffic . . . In January 1854 a through traffic arrangement was made via first class vessels between Milford Haven and Waterford.' Such a steamship route from

---

* The poor man had but a short tenure of his post and did not live to see the opening of the line to Waterford. Crossing the gangway from ship to shore at Holyhead when visiting England, he slipped, fell in the water and was drowned.

Bury type 2-2-2 built by Stothert & Slaughter of Bristol in 1847 for the W&LR, similar to the one shown in the photograph below. Note the primitive buffers, high firebox with safety valve on top, absence of a cab and hand brakes on the tender only.   *Irish Railway Record Society*

The earliest known photograph of an Irish railway scene: a 2-2-2 shunts a train at Clonmel on the W&LR in 1858. The six engines of this class were withdrawn between 1860 and 1862.
          Irish Railway Record Society

South West Wales to southern parts of Ireland shortened the distance considerably as compared with the journey via Holyhead and Dublin, and both companies were therefore interested in co-operating in order to capture traffic. The GWR was later to agree to making substantial repayments of money to the W&LR from the sums which the latter paid to it as its proportion of fares and charges on through traffic in order to keep the latter company going as a traffic artery. A paragraph in the 1855 *Shareholders' Guide* quotes the then Chairman of the W&LR waxing lyrical over the possibilities of the new ferry service.

> I am informed that the works are rapidly being pushed forward by the South Wales (Railway) to what will be one of the finest harbours in the world when completed, which it must be in a few months. It cannot be supposed that the English lines will let slip from them the chief traffic of the South of Ireland, which must reach them over our railway. The matter is but a question of time. We want to go into opposition with no other line. We are preparing to live on amicable terms with all; but firmly we are determined to maintain that traffic which legitimately belongs to our line. Fancy for a moment what a field for provision traffic South Wales alone opens up for us. She has a great mining population, well paid* - they must be well fed. Her riches are chiefly in the bowels of the earth, ours on the surface. Who can supply them with beef and mutton and bacon and butter as we can? In part return we are prepared to take from them with pleasure, and distribute through the country, if nothing else, at least their coals in great abundance, while the passengers who travel over their bold and interesting line will continue to find no lack of attraction as they pass by the quieter but not less lovely scenery of the valley of the Suir. Such are our hopes for the future.
>
> (H.W. Massey, Chairman: 30th August, 1854.)

However, in 1857 the enthusiasm was more muted, for another direct steamer service had begun to operate from South Wales to Cork, by-passing Waterford altogether, and in 1860 a pained comment in the *Shareholders' Guide* recorded the company's displeasure at the apparently deliberate provision of better boats for the Cork service than for that to Waterford, which it regarded as a breach of previously-given undertakings. In 1870 discussions took place with the GWR (which had now absorbed the South Wales Railway) that resulted in the English company offering to

> . . . make up to your company, by way of rebate on traffic of every description passing or forwarded via Waterford and Milford, and interchanged between the two companies, such a sum as when added to the net balance of your revenue account will make up to your shareholders a dividend, for the first three years of the agreement, at the rate of £2 per cent, and for the remaining term of the agreement at the rate of £3 per cent per annum on your ordinary share capital, your company retaining, now and in future, all profits which may be earned by them in excess of these rates.
>
> (Bradshaw's *Shareholders' Guide* 1871, p. 302)

This seemingly generous offer of course owed much to self-interest on the part of the GWR. If the W&LR were to go out of business traffic would certainly be lost by the GWR, while if on the other hand it had fallen into the hands of the GS&WR, which operated in co-operation with the London & North Western Railway, a certain amount of traffic would be lost to the Holyhead and Kingstown route. The GWR Board must have been well aware that a number

---

* One wonders what made him suppose this.

of W&LR Directors, including the Chairman, favoured coming to an understanding with the GS&WR to replace competition by co-operation as far as was possible. The agreement with the GWR was duly made but opposition began to simmer within the Board and among the shareholders, which eventually broke out into violent dissension.

It may seem surprising that large numbers of shareholders should favour the demise of the company in which they had invested their money, but it was increasingly obvious that the W&LR would not be able to pay its way if it tried to go it alone; the optimism of earlier days had now evaporated. A merger with the GS&WR would be preceded by negotiations in which the financial interests of all shareholders would have to be considered. As hard a bargain as possible would have to be driven. The question was: with whom to drive the bargain? Co-operation with the largest of the Irish railway companies seemed to some a safer policy than co-operation with the English giant which in return for favours was bound to insist on some measure of control over the affairs of the smaller company. In the February 1872 half-yearly meeting the simmering dissensions came to the boil. To quote from an article in the (October 1975) *Journal* of the Irish Railway Record Society:

> As the matter was very much one of the likely future return on capital, Malcomson obtained an undertaking from the GS&WR to guarantee a W&LR dividend of 4 per cent. However, the pro-GWR party persuaded the GWR Chairman, Sir Daniel Gooch, to improve the GWR offer of traffic rebates to permit a similar return. At the February meeting (at which accusations were made amid 'fearful uproar') some of the pro-Malcomson directors were displaced, and in disgust Malcomson resigned as Chairman . . . On 18th April the amended agreement with the GWR was signed by the directors and it was approved by the shareholders on 29th May. It was for 21 years, and came into force on 1st July. It involved through fares and charges, interchange of traffic, connecting services at Waterford and New Milford, and the payment, out of a 'Joint Fund', of sufficient rebates to permit a 4 per cent dividend on W&LR ordinary shares. The Irish company was to provide, to GWR satisfaction, a service of connecting trains to and from Waterford, which were not to be mixed trains. The GWR was to run a suitable daily (excluding Sunday) steamboat service between Waterford and New Milford. In July a GWR engineer . . . came over to inspect the W&LR system, and on 1st September new services were introduced with third class carriages attached, for the first time, to all trains. Earlier, in February, the GWR had taken over the New Milford-Waterford steamer service from Jackson & Co. and had announced that four new powerful steamers were to be built, at a cost of £100,000.

For the moment the shareholders acquiesced in the deal, presumably on the principle that the devil you know is better than the devil you don't know. What was chiefly at issue was whether or not investors would get a satisfactory return on their money. However, quarrelling broke out again in 1874. The new steamboat service organised by the GWR and the system of connecting passengers-only trains had begun between Waterford and Limerick. What did not eventuate was the promised regular payment of dividends which the new arrangements with the GWR had supposedly guaranteed. In 1873 the GWR had withheld payment, which, so it maintained, was only due if the W&LR 'working ratio' had remained at the agreed figure, i.e. if 47 per cent of the net receipts had been sufficient to meet expenses, leaving 3 per cent to go to reserves and 50 per cent to be available for payment of dividends. In fact the W&LR required 54 per cent for its working ratio. The pro-GWR party on the Board favoured persuading that company to continue to honour its agreement despite the increase in the expense of working the line, and was willing to accede to the GWR's further demands that it should be allowed to control the W&LR's income and expenditure, and even appoint executive officers - demands which certainly seem rather drastic - but the pro-GS&WR party, led by a newcomer to the Board, O.F. Lombard, were infuriated and blamed the lack of dividend on bad management. A crisis was staved off by the payment of a 3 per cent dividend for the half-year ending in February 1873, when it was hoped that the GWR would pay up after all, but the following September shareholders were told that the dividend was being deferred until the dispute with the GWR had been settled.

All hell now broke loose, and matters were made even worse when the Chairman, Abraham Stephens, refused to recognise the status of one Board member on the grounds that at the time of his election he had not held sufficient shares to qualify him as a candidate. So deep was the division and so great was the bad feeling that the 'rebels' held their own meetings and made written protests in the Board's minute book. They in turn were accused of holding meetings irregularly whose proceedings had no legal force. The rebels, at an 'illegal' meeting in Dublin in October, lambasted the loyalists and called on Stephens and his friends to resign (which they refused to do) and for a Committee of Investigation to be established (which request was ignored.) Meanwhile the GWR, watching events from a distance, in November informed Stephens that it was prepared to relax its requirements and agree that the W&LR might have a higher working ratio.

This did not immediately placate the rebels. In a shareholders' meeting in January 1875 the pro-GWR Directors, including the Chairman Stephens, were ousted, four of the opposite party being elected to take their places. The Committee of Investigation also began its work, and a new Chairman, Thomas Synnott of Dublin, was elected to the Chair. It was given out that the troubles recently experienced, and the threat of restricted dividends, had been the consequences of poor management, and that things were now expected slowly to improve. The former Secretary, J.F. Nichols, who had been dismissed for non co-operation by the now-ousted GWR faction, was reinstated and offered the position of Assistant General Manager, which he felt it prudent to decline. A number of new executive officers were appointed. Board meetings were now held in Dublin. The advances made by the GWR were responded to, but negotiations were to be long and protracted. Meanwhile the line slowly became more prosperous financially; the dividend was up to 3 per cent again by 1877, after which it fluctuated; however, at the end of the decade the company appeared to be in better shape than before, while the GWR rebates did not fail as they had done previously. But, at the start of the next decade a jarring note appeared in relations with the GWR. The latter during 1879 and 1880 had been interpreting its agreement with the W&LR differently from what the latter had expected, and had not paid over to the Irish company the amounts which the

Waterford & Central Ireland train at Waterford on 5th September, 1900. The locomotive is 2-4-0 No. 5, built by Stothert & Slaughter in 1852, and which ran as Waterford & Limerick Railway No. 24 between 1860 and 1866.   *LCGB/Ken Nunn Collection H740*

WL&WR 0-6-0 No. 49 *Dreadnought*, designed by J.G. Robinson, built by Dübs & Co. in 1895 and sen here at Listowel on 3rd September, 1901.   *LCGB/Ken Nunn Collection*

WL&WR 2-4-0 No. 20 *Galteemoore*, designed by J.G. Robinson and built by Dübs & Co. in 1892, approaching Limerick on a goods train 3rd September, 1900.   *LCGB/Ken Nunn Collection H749*

Fairbairn 2-4-0 No. 11, built in 1853, standing outside the locomotive works at Limerick about 1895. This engine became GS&WR No. 264 in 1900 but was withdrawn the following year.

L&GRP

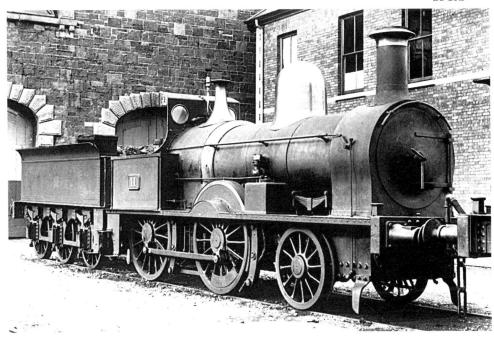

0-4-0 No. 29 is seen at Limerick on 3rd September, 1900. Note the coaches in the background, with oil-lamp caps over the compartments. The engine will take the train out only as far as the check cabin, where it will reverse for Foynes or Tralee.   *LCGB/Ken Nunn Collection H751*

WL&WR 4-4-0 No. 53 *Jubilee* designed by J.G. Robinson and built by Kitson & Co. in 1896, photographed at Sligo on 3rd September, 1900 still in full Robinson crimson livery.

LCGB/Ken Nunn Collection H759

latter thought was its due. Legal opinion was sought and the matter eventually went to arbitration. The finding was in favour of the W&LR, which was awarded £5,200.

During its whole independent existence the W&LR had to keep a tight rein on its finances, being niggardly in the matter of wages and salaries and economising where it could. An examination of its published accounts, which are set out in full in the *Shareholders' Guide* from 1877 to 1899, show considerable fluctuations both in gross receipts and net income while the Capital Receipts and Expenditure Account shows a deficit continuously between 1886 and 1899 which sometimes approached and once exceeded £50,000. Throughout this time the W&LR was working several other lines as well as its own, but these did not yield the desired profits, whether they were being worked by the W&LR or whether they had been taken into the latter's ownership.

After 1890 the GWR began to re-think its Irish policy. The traffic between South Wales and Waterford had not been up to expectations; relations with the W&LR had been difficult at times; financially the latter did not seem to be doing very well. Would the GS&WR perhaps make a more satisfactory partner? Discreet approaches were made to the latter line, but as yet the latter had no access to Waterford and for the moment nothing came of the proposal. But soon afterwards one line's extremity proved another's opportunity. The Waterford, Dungarvan & Lismore Railway, which had now reached Fermoy where it made an end-on junction with the G&SWR's branch from Mallow, had been in financial straits for some years and now asked the latter company whether it would be willing to take it over. The latter was only too ready to acquiesce, for now the desired access to Waterford was forthcoming, by a route which would shorten the distance to Cork by some 16 miles. By August 1898 the negotiations were complete and the GWR was brought into the picture. This company was not only ready to co-operate with the GS&WR in regard to the South Wales-Waterford service, but was also planning a new route from Fishguard to Rosslare. A former Fishguard and Rosslare Railways and Harbours Company' was revived; the GWR undertook to build a branch from its own Swansea-Milford Haven line to link it with Fishguard, to manage the latter port and provide a steamer service to Rosslare, while the GS&WR undertook for its part to manage the harbour at Rosslare and build a line to link that port with Waterford. Once this had been achieved most of the passenger traffic would by-pass Waterford Harbour altogether.

The W&LR could of course do nothing about this new development except bow to the inevitable. It had long been accepting rebates from the GWR which would now cease, and without them it could not survive. So approaches were made to the GS&WR for an amalgamation of the two lines, and were soon concluded. The smaller company drove the best bargain it could, the GS&WR agreeing to guarantee existing shareholders a 2½ per cent dividend. Four of the Directors joined the Board of the GS&WR. On 1st January, 1901 the Waterford, Limerick & Western Railway (as it had now become) ceased to exist. Having first worked and then absorbed so many smaller lines, it was now swallowed up itself, making a large meal which the GS&WR digested with difficulty.

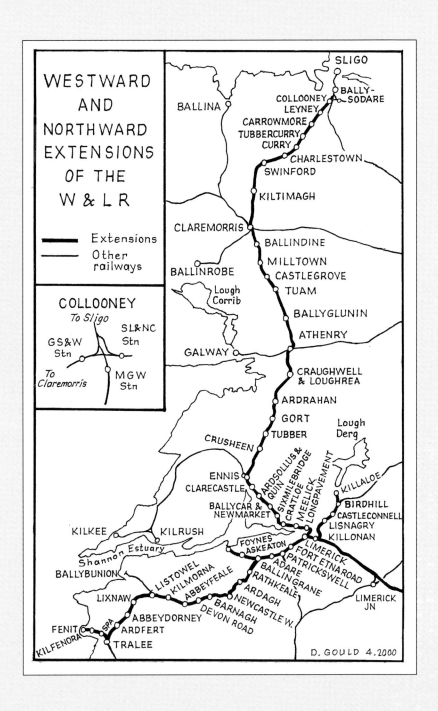

WESTWARD
AND
NORTHWARD
EXTENSIONS
OF THE
W & L R

━━━━ Extensions
──── Other
        railways

COLLOONEY

To Sligo

GS&W   SL&NC
Stn   Stn

To
Claremorris   MGW
                    Stn

SLIGO
BALLY-
SODARE
COLLOONEY
LEYNEY
CARROWMORE
TUBBERCURRY
CURRY
CHARLESTOWN
SWINFORD
KILTIMAGH
BALLINA
CLAREMORRIS
BALLINDINE
MILLTOWN
CASTLEGROVE
TUAM
BALLYGLUNIN
ATHENRY
BALLINROBE
Lough
Corrib
GALWAY
CRAUGHWELL
& LOUGHREA
ARDRAHAN
GORT
TUBBER
Lough
Derg
CRUSHEEN
KILLALOE
ENNIS
CLARECASTLE
ARDSOLLUS &
QUIN
SIXMILEBRIDGE
CRATLOE
MEELICK
LONGPAVEMENT
BIRDHILL
CASTLECONNELL
LISNAGRY
KILLONAN
BALLYCAR &
NEWMARKET
KILKEE
KILRUSH
FOYNES
ASKEATON
LIMERICK
FORT ETNA ROAD
PATRICKSWELL
Shannon Estuary
BALLYBUNION
LISTOWEL
KILMORNA
ABBEYFEALE
ADARE
BALLINGRANE
RATHKEALE
ARDAGH
NEWCASTLE W.
LIMERICK
JN
LIXNAW
BARNAGH
DEVON ROAD
FENIT
KILFENORA
SPA
ABBEYDORNEY
ARDFERT
TRALEE

D. GOULD 4.2000

Chapter Five

Lines Worked by the W&LR
East and West of Limerick

Almost from the time of its own completion the Waterford & Limerick Railway undertook the working of other smaller newly established lines, one after the other. This was something that commonly happened in the days when enthusiasm for the railway as the best means of taking passengers and goods over long distances often outran realism on the part of promoters, who soon realised that the cost of purchasing their own locomotives and rolling stock over and above the expense of their fixed installations was beyond their capabilities. Another company would then be approached and a bargain of some sort would be struck by which the latter would supply engines, coaches and men to work them, either at an agreed percentage of the line's receipts or for a fixed annual sum. Dependent in this way on the operations of the larger company, the smaller one often found in course of time that the most advantageous step to take on its shareholders' behalf was to sell itself to its larger neighbour and lose its separate identity. In some such manner the original multiplicity of small railways in the British Isles eventually became very much reduced. In the course of less than 50 years the Waterford and Limerick, having gathered into its empire by attachment or absorption as many as 11 different concerns, grew to a huge size and eventually vanished into the maw of an even larger neighbour.

The first line which it undertook to work, soon after its own opening, was the Limerick & Foynes Railway which, incorporated by Act of Parliament in 1853, was opened to Rathcale (Ballingrane) on 12th July, 1856 and throughout on 29th April, 1858. It had influential supporters. William Dargan, who undertook its construction, and who had been responsible for building many Irish railways, including, as has been seen, the W&LR, himself contributed as much as one-third of the share capital. Another Director was the Earl of Dunraven, a large landowner in County Kerry, who was hopeful that Foynes, on the south bank of the Shannon estuary, might become a port for steamers making the Atlantic crossing, which it never did. Dargan, who set his sights lower, saw it as a terminus for craft plying on the Shannon, and after the line had been completed he organised steamer services between Limerick and Foynes so that excursionists could travel one way by water and return by land, or vice versa. However, he did not long remain to influence the company's fortunes, but sold his shares to William Malcomson after the latter had become Chairman of the W&LR; Lord Dunraven did the same. Soon afterwards, in 1873, the W&LR took the line over completely.

The Limerick & Foynes Railway left Limerick station at the south end on a sharp curve before heading south-west across easy pastoral country, with stations at Patricks Well (later spelt Patrickswell) Adare and Ballingrane, where it turned north-west towards the Shannon Estuary and Foynes, 26½ miles from Limerick (later a halt was opened at Kildobbin between Patricks Well and Adare). Three trains were run each way daily during most of the year, reduced to two in the winter. The time taken was about an hour and a quarter. This

A view looking towards Limerick at Patrickswell on 7th June, 1964 with 'J15' class 0-6-0 No. 186 on the Irish Railway Record Society, Railway Correspondence and Travel Society and Stephenson Locomotive Society joint Irish Tour of 1964.   *R.M. Casserley*

'J15' class 0-6-0 No. 106 is seen at Adare with the 4.15 pm Foynes-Limerick train.
R.M. Casserley

Ballingrane in 1933, with the line from Foynes coming straight in from the left, and that from Tralee curving in at the centre. *L&GRP*

A view along the platform at Ballingrane on 22nd April, 1955, looking towards Foynes.
R.M. Casserley

Ballingrane station from the road approach on 7th June, 1964.   *R.M. Casserley*

The Saxby & Farmer signal box on the up platform at Ballingrane in 1933.   *L&GRP*

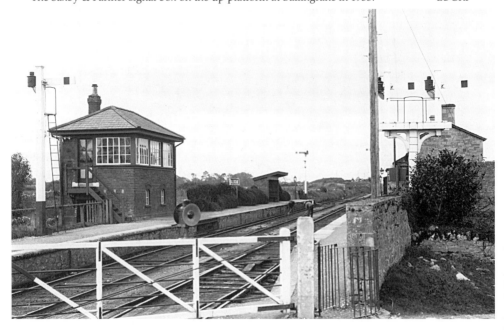

Askeaton station looking towards Foynes on 22nd April, 1955.   *R.M. Casserley*

Foynes station viewed from the buffer stops on 22nd April, 1955.   *R.M. Casserley*

The engine shed at Foynes with 'J15' class 0-6-0 No. 106 alongside on 22nd April, 1955.
H.C. Casserley

The single road shed at Killaloe, with ex-GSWR 0-6-0 No. 106 on 18th June, 1939.
W.A. Camwell

pattern of service lasted until 1867 when (as seen below) it was altered to the detriment of Foynes-bound passengers, to take twice as long. By now Foynes had become the terminus of a short branch and was of less relative importance than before. However, services were to improve after the turn of the century, by which time the line had come under GS&WR ownership, when quicker connections were made at Ballingrane; in 1910 the time allowed in either direction had fallen to between 73 and 80 minutes, and in 1922 some trains were faster still. However, on the eve of World War II the three-a-day-each-way pattern had been reduced to two, and in 1963 the line was closed to passenger traffic altogether, though still remaining open for some freight traffic.

On 1st August, 1862 the Cork & Limerick Direct Railway was opened from Rathluirc (then called Charleville) on the Cork line, into Limerick. The junction was west of Patricks Well on the Foynes branch. Running powers were granted by the L&FR but in fact a separate track was laid alongside it for ¾ mile to the south end of the station, where the GS&WR, which always worked the service, set up a goods depot. The separate 'Cork & Limerick Direct' track was first used on 30th April, 1863; its right to a platform in the W&LR station was awarded at an arbitration by T.E. Harrison, Engineer-in-Chief of the English North Eastern Railway. In 1905 a connection was put in to the 'Foynes Loop'.

In 1858 the W&LR undertook the working of the Limerick & Castleconnell Railway (L&CR). This line, incorporated by Act of Parliament in 1856, diverged northwards from the W&LR at Killonan, 4½ miles from Limerick, followed the eastern side of the Shannon valley to Castleconnell, to which point it was opened in 1858, and a few years later was extended to Killaloe at the outflow from Lough Derg into the Shannon. Seven years later it was further extended to a deep water quay a mile or so northwards, at which river steamers could berth. The W&LR had been interested in this line from the start, as had also another of the principal Irish lines, the Midland & Great Western, which purchased shares in it and organised a service of river steamers from Athlone, some 80 miles north of Killaloe along the middle Shannon and Lough Derg, to connect with its trains. The W&LR ran the line, but it proved to be somewhat of a pig in a poke, yielding annual receipts of under £200 each year until taken over in 1872. The services it offered were correspondingly few and poor, with only two trains each way daily.

However, in June 1864 the GS&WR completed a line from Ballybrophy through Nenagh to Birdhill, on the L&CR, which gave it a second access to Limerick in addition to the one through Limerick Junction, and the branch line then assumed a greater importance. Killaloe now had a shorter link with the GS&WR main line to Dublin by way of Birdhill, and eventually, after being taken into GS&WR ownership in 1901, the line had a shuttle service between those two places, with as many as eight trains each way daily by 1910. However, patronage fell off during and after World War I; the line was closed to passenger traffic between Birdhill and Killaloe in 1931, and to all traffic in 1944.

Another railway worked for a time by the W&LR was the Waterford & Kilkenny Railway (W&KR), incorporated in 1845, and completed to Dunkitt Junction, which was shortly to be opened by the W&LR, on 18th May, 1853. A joint single line into Waterford was opened on 11th September, 1854, to a joint terminus on the north bank of the Suir, said to have been brought by William

Rathkeale station looking east in 1933.   *L&GRP*

Rathkeale station looking west in 1931.   *L&GRP*

Dargan from the 1853 Dublin Exhibition. Joint use of the line was unsatisfactory, and the W&LR laid 1¼ mile of parallel line for the use of the W&KR. The latter, with a Board composed mainly of English Directors who had no direct experience of local needs, and with most of its shares held in England, was an ill-starred venture, one of a number of lines centring on Kilkenny which were mooted during the early 1840s. Building began at Kilkenny in 1847, and Thomastown was reached in May 1845, but Dunkitt Junction, where the line joined the W&LR, not until May 1853. For a while the railway tried to run itself, but made a complete hash of things. A contemporary comment in the *Irish Railway Gazette* did not err on the side of kindness. 'By the grossest mismanagement, by jobbery, by a succession of engineering blunders and a consistency of reckless expenditure [it] has been driven almost to bankruptcy'. At one point relations became so bad between the two companies that the W&LR took the W&KR to court over the latter's refusal to pay its share towards the establishment of a new and more conveniently sited station at Waterford. This was in 1868, and by the time an arbitration award was made the two companies were having nothing to do with each other. The W&KR was found responsible for improperly withholding money due to the W&LR, and was required to pay the latter 5 per cent of the shortfall of £14,462 each year in perpetuity.

The W&KR had a locomotive shed at Waterford, but repairs were carried out at Kilkenny. In 1860 the W&LR agreed to work the W&KR for five years, and took over its six locomotives, renumbering them in its own stock as Nos. 22-7. Five years later the W&LR refused to renew the Agreement, and from 1st July, 1866 the W&KR resumed its own working. Only five engines were returned by the W&LR; the three original W&KR 4-2-2T engines had gone before the Agreement was made, and the one retained seems to have been Fairbairn 0-4-2 No. 1 which continued to work on the W&LR until 1875. The W&KR in 1868 became the Waterford & Central Ireland Railway (along with some other lines) and finally part of the G&SWR from 1900.

In 1861 Parliament authorised the building of the Rathkeale and Newcastle Junction line, which was in effect a south-westwards extension of the Limerick and Foynes line, diverging at Ballingrane. Like the L&FR it was worked by the W&LR from the start. Both these railways each invested £5,000 in it. Constructed by J. Hargreaves of Cork, it was completed in October 1866, though services did not actually commence until 1st January, 1867, when a water tower for replenishing locomotive tanks was installed at Newcastle West station. This line continued the L&FR westwards, and the W&LR, when organising the train service, introduced an awkwardness so far as passengers from Limerick to Foynes were concerned. It was desired to serve both Foynes and Newcastle West in a single operation from Limerick with the same locomotive and set of coaches for the sake of economy, so that passengers from Limerick to Foynes had to leave the train at Ballingrane and wait there until the train had proceeded to Newcastle West, reversed and come back, before they rejoined it and went on to Foynes. Hence the outward journey to Foynes, instead of taking an hour and a quarter, took twice that time. People travelling from Newcastle West to Limerick were similarly inconvenienced. One wonders whether de-training was insisted upon at Ballingrane when the weather was bleak.

'J15' class 0-6-0 No. 106 is seen at Newcastle West on 14th July, 1934 with the 5.30 pm Tralee to Limerick train, after reversal. Note the station nameboard just gives 'Newcastle'.*H.C. Casserley*

'J15' class 0-6-0 No. 175 is seen at Newcastle West on the 5.30 pm Limerick to Tralee train on 5th July, 1950. Engines were allowed ten minutes to run-round and turn on the turntable.

T.J. Edgington

Newcastle West station from the station approach on 5th June, 1961.   *R.M. Casserley*

The station building at Newcastle West viewed from the buffer stops on 7th June, 1964, after the removal of the overall roof.   *R.M. Casserley*

Newcastle West signal box, of the type built by the Gloucester Wagon Co. in 1879-1884, on 16th April, 1955 with the new box under construction on the left.   *R.M. Casserley*

The new signal box at Newcastle West on 8th June, 1964, looking away from the station.
H.C. Casserley

A Tralee to Limerick train entering Listowel about 1900, with two of Robinson's bogie coaches included in the make-up. Behind the signal box, on the extreme right, can be seen part of the Listowel & Ballybunion Railway's carriage shed.   *L&GRP*

In 1880 a further extension of this line took place with the opening of the Limerick & Kerry Railway from Newcastle West to Tralee, one of the principal towns in Kerry and the furthest place of any size from Dublin. The W&LR began to work it as soon as it had been completed. This continuation line was quite lengthy, and needed to negotiate a range of hills, so that gradients on either side of the summit at Barnagh, 538 feet above sea level, were of the order of 1 in 50 to 1 in 70, making a difficult section between two relatively easy ones where the line ran across fairly flat country. The principal station between Newcastle West and Tralee was Listowel, where anyone desirous both of seeing the Atlantic Ocean and also having a unique railway experience could alight and board one of the monorail trains to Ballybunion. Built on the Lartigue system, with double-boilered locomotives and coaches slung pannier-wise across a single central rail some four feet above the ground and held in position by triangular supports, the Listowel & Ballybunion Railway connected the two places by a train service taking 40 minutes for the 9¼ miles with one intermediate stop. Built in 1888, it lasted until 1924. It never paid its way and by 1900 was in the hands of the Official Receiver. When the Irish railway system was unified under one company in 1924 its doom was sealed; it remains as a memory and a source of amusing anecdotes. One would have liked to write more about it, but as it was never worked by the W&LR a digression at length would be irrelevant.*

* For a history of this line see *The Listowel & Ballybunion Railway* by A.T. Newham and revised by Michael Foster, published by The Oakwood Press. Chapter 8 of *One Hundred and Fifty Years of Irish Railways*, P.F. Mulligan, also has a full and entertaining account of this railway.

'Flower' class 2-4-0 No. 30 *Lily*, built by Vulcan Foundry in 1874, calls at Listowel about 1900 with a train for Limerick. The passengers on the footbridge are not heading for the monorail train to Ballybunion as this was over to the right. *L&GRP*

The IRRS, RCTS and SLS joint railtour, heading towards Newcastle, is captured at Listowel with 'J15' class locomotives Nos. 186 and 130 on 8th June, 1964. *H.C. Casserley*

'J15' class 0-6-0 No. 106 is seen at Tralee prior to working the 5.30 pm to Limerick on 14th July, 1934. Note the fine train-shed roof and the waiting 'taxi'. *H.C. Casserley*

'J15' class 0-6-0 No. 141 at rest by the water tower at Tralee in 1933. *L&GRP*

Midland Great Western Railway 'J26' class 0-6-0T No. 560 is seen on a special for Fenit at Spa on 5th June, 1961.   *R.M. Casserley*

'J15' class 0-6-0 No. 102 with the 1.15 pm to Tralee at Fenit on 13th July, 1934. This was the most westerly station to which W&LR trains worked.   *H.C. Casserley*

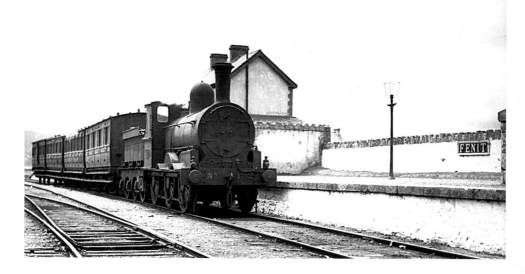

Fenit looking towards the pier on 5th June, 1961 with the special headed by MGWR
'J26' class 0-6-0T No. 560.   *H.C. Casserley*

The Limerick & Kerry Railway remained independent until it lost its separate
identity when taken over by the GS&WR in 1901. The service provided was
three daily trains in both directions between Limerick and Tralee, reversing at
Newcastle West and taking 3½ hours for the 70¼ miles, with 15 intermediate
stops, that at Newcastle West being prolonged since here reversal was needed.
After 1901 there was a gradual speed-up, some trains taking as little as three
hours.   The line continued to carry passengers until 1963, and freight
subsequently until 1975, when it was closed to all traffic.

The W&LR's westernmost outpost now calls for a mention. The fishing
village of Fenit lies eight miles west of Tralee and has a deep water quay where
fishing vessels may berth. With the aid of a grant from the public purse a line
was built connecting the two places in 1887, and the W&LR undertook to work
it. Traffic was disappointingly small, and despite quite a frequent service with
two intermediate stops it attracted so little custom that Official Receiver
eventually had to take charge; however, the W&LR continued to provide trains,
and after the latter's merger with the GS&WR this line perpetuated the
working. Fenit trains used the old station at Limerick, but others used the
GS&WR one from 1901.   In 1910 there were three westbound and four
eastbound services, taking some 25 minutes each way.   Regular passenger
services ceased at the end of 1934 but excursions were occasionally run until
demand for them fell off. Since 1975 traffic has been limited to occasional
freight trains connecting with the arrival of ships.

Fethard station from the station approach on 7th June, 1964.   *R.M. Casserley*

Fethard station looking towards Clonmel on 23rd April, 1955.   *H.C. Casserley*

Finally one turns to the grandiosely-named Southern of Ireland Railway - more informatively the Thurles to Clonmel branch, which was incorporated by Act of Parliament in July 1865. As an independent concern it was dogged by misfortune from the start. Money was not forthcoming in sufficient amounts, and perhaps the fact that the Chairman of the company and most of the Directors were resident in England and not in local touch with the project was a hindrance. Construction went ahead very slowly, with many intermissions, being undertaken piecemeal, first by one contractor, then by another. Not until 23rd June, 1879 was the first section opened, the 8¾ miles from Clonmel to Fethard; a year later Thurles was reached. The W&LR had already agreed to work the line and had bought shares in it; curiously, no mention appears of the working arrangements in the latter company's reports in the *Shareholders' Guide*. It continued to provide the locomotives and rolling stock until its own amalgamation with the GS&WR at the end of the century. Two passenger trains, a mixed train and a goods train operated in each direction. There were no through trains to Dublin, connections being made at Thurles; the waits between trains were sometimes very lengthy. Schedules were arranged not so much for the convenience of passengers as to enable as few locomotives as possible to be used. One engine was used to haul all the passenger and mixed services, the station pilot at Clonmel being employed on the double-journey goods train.

After the amalgamation of the W&LR and the GS&WR the latter took over the pattern of working without much change. In 1910 there were still three passenger trains each way daily and this was still the case shortly before the unification of the Republic's railways in 1925. The line suffered considerable damage during the 'Troubles' of 1922-1923, bridges and signal boxes being destroyed and permanent way being pulled up in eight places. It was patrolled by armoured cars manned by members of the Irish Free State Army, and one of them was on one occasion forced to surrender by Irish Republican Army irregulars. Once the fighting was over the branch was speedily repaired by the Railway Defence Corps.

The 'Southern of Ireland' was never absorbed by the GS&WR, but who actually owned it in its latter days is something of a mystery, and the actual outcome in 1924-1925, when its inclusion in the unified Great Southern Railway was sought, verges on the incredible, as detailed in the *Railway Magazine* (May 1957):

> It was found that nobody could furnish information about offices, officers, directors, shareholders or creditors of the company, and the consideration of an absorption scheme for the line was postponed for six months to allow advertisements to be published. Nobody came forward as a result of these, however, and the absorption scheme was duly settled on 17th November, 1925, the line thereafter being an integral part of the GSR.

This disappearance into limbo of a complete financial organisation is no doubt to be explained by its having gone into Receivership in 1855 and never having emerged as a viable company again. The people who could have declared an interest were probably all in their graves.

Ex-GS&WR 'D12' class 4-4-0 No. 307 on a Clonmel-Thurles goods train at Laffansbridge for Killenaule on 23rd May, 1958.   *T.J. Edgington*

Laffansbridge station on 7th June, 1964 looking towards Thurles. Tickets and timetables called the station Laffans Bridge.   *R.M. Casserley*

Horse & Jockey station looking towards Thurles on 23rd April, 1955.   *R.M. Casserley*

Successful or not as a business concern, the line certainly filled a need during the 19th and early 20th centuries, for Clonmel is and was the largest centre of population in County Tipperary, a bustling market town with local industries. However, its only other connections with Dublin, by way of Waterford or Limerick Junction, were very roundabout, and the line to Thurles shortened the journey to the capital considerably. At the time when the article from which the above extract was taken was published the railway was still in use, and the journey time from Clonmel to Dublin and vice versa was only a little over three hours. However, the all-conquering motor vehicle was now beginning to take traffic away, and the need for retrenchment obliged the Irish Transport authority, Coras Iompair Eireann, to close the line to passenger traffic in 1963 and to all traffic in 1967.

Until 1908 the W&LR station at Waterford was called Waterford North. This was because the Waterford, Dungarvan & Lismore Railway, opened on 12th August, 1872, had built a South station, south of the river and west of the town. On 30th August, 1906 a spur from Grace Dieu Junction, 1½ miles west of Waterford North, was opened across the river to that station. No passenger trains ran to South station after 31st January, 1908, but it remained in use as a goods station.

The third station in Waterford, known as Manor, was opened in 1853 for trains to Tramore on the coast; no part of the Waterford & Tramore Railway was ever connected to the other lines, though proposals to do so were made from time to time. It closed in 1960.

Ardsollus & Quin station view looking towards Ennis on 22nd April, 1955.   *H.C. Casserley*

Ennis station looking north on 30th April, 1938 with the engine shed on the left and the Gloucester Wagon Co. signal box of 1879-84 period in the centre.   *W.A. Camwell*

Chapter Six

Lines Worked by the W&LR
North of Limerick

The fact that the Waterford & Limerick Railway had already built a substantial station in Limerick was an obvious invitation to any other railway, subsequently constructed to connect that city with any other part of Ireland, to use it instead of building one of its own. There were two disincentives, however, if the railway were to serve the regions north of the city; one was that the existing station looked to the south-east, so that a considerable detour around the eastern side of Limerick would have to be undertaken; the other was the necessity to bridge the Shannon at a point before it was widening out to reach its estuary. The first line to be proposed in this direction, to link Limerick with Ennis, the chief town in County Clare, was the Limerick, Ennis & Clare Junction Railway, sanctioned by Parliament in 1846. This, had it been built, would not have crossed the river at Limerick, but would have extended farther along the north bank upstream as far as Killaloe, here to link up with a proposed branch of the GS&WR which would diverge with the latter's main line to Cork at or near Ballybrophy and pass through Roscrea and Nenagh. Shortage of funds at a time of severe agrarian distress prevented both lines from being constructed. In 1853, however, a modified and less ambitious scheme was approved by Parliament for a line between Limerick and Ennis. Construction began, but the contractor withdrew from the undertaking and William Dargan was asked to complete it. At the beginning of 1859 the greater part of the line was finished, including a many-spanned girder bridge across the Shannon some two miles upstream from the city; however, the Board of Trade's inspector found faults in the construction of the bridge which it took two months to rectify. On 26th March of that year the first train carrying passengers ran from Limerick W&LR station as far as Clarecastle, two miles short of Ennis itself; soon afterwards the final stretch into the town was completed.

Arrangements had been made for the W&LR to work the line, and for a few weeks it did so, but so many complaints were made about the timings of the services and their infrequency that at the end of the year the Limerick & Ennis Railway hired several second hand locomotives and carriages from a source in Dublin and took over the running of the line itself from November 1859. Finding that it could not do this satisfactorily, the company disposed of its newly-purchased engines and coaches and turned again to the W&LR in May 1861. After some negotiations the latter again undertook the working, charging 43 per cent of gross receipts, in return for which it ran three passenger trains each way daily, each taking 85 minutes to make the journey with stops at the intermediate stations of Longpavement, Cratloe, Sixmilebridge, Ballycar, Ardsollus & Quin and Clarecastle. The service appears now to have been found satisfactory, for its pattern continued until the W&LR took the line into ownership in 1893, and by 1898 the time for most trains between Limerick and Ennis had been reduced to the even hour, two of them being through trains to

A view of Ennis station from the north in 1931. The 3 ft gauge West Clare Railway line to Miltown Malbay left the main line here. One of the narrow gauge trains can be seen on the right.
L&GRP

The 9.05 am train from Claremorris to Limerick calls at Ennis on 21st June, 1939. Class 'G3' 2-4-0 No. 276 was originally W&LR No. 23 *Slieve na Mon*, built by Dübs in 1892.
R.W. Miller Collection

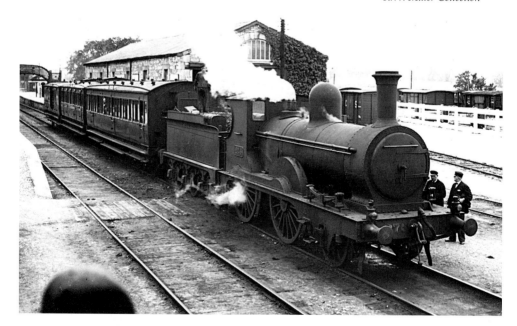

Sligo.   Following the amalgamation of 1901 the GS&WR made further improvements both in schedules and frequency, and by 1910 there were five trains each way, the fastest taking just over an hour.

The course of the line is over level country for the first two-thirds of its 24¾ miles.   Leaving the main W&LR line just under a mile from Limerick, it curves round to the east of the city, crosses the Shannon by a large girder bridge and then bears to the west to circumvent the natural obstacle of Woodcock Hill, a 1,600 ft outlier of the Slieve Bernagh range. West of Cratloe it bears to the north, then turns north-west across undulating country, rises near Newmarket to a short tunnel and then falls to cross the river Fergus, a tributary of the Shannon Estuary, at Clarecastle; Ennis is two miles further on.   At its half-way point the railway passes within sight of the Shannon International Airport, which lies on a flat peninsula east of the outflow of the Fergus; its neighbourhood is now becoming a focus for light industries. It will be noticed that the present tense is used in this paragraph, for the line is still in being, and although passenger services were discontinued in 1976, in 1993 they were experimentally re-introduced, and continue to run; from Tuesday to Friday the fast morning through train from Limerick to Dublin starts instead at Ennis at 7.30 am, leaves Limerick at 8.20, gets to Dublin at 10.20 am, leaves there in the evening at 5.40 pm, arrives at Limerick at 7.45 and terminates at Ennis at 8.30 pm. With no intermediate stops, since the stations have now been closed, the journey over the branch now takes 40 minutes, faster than ever before, though not exactly at express speed since the track is not yet up to express train standard.

Beyond Ennis two railways between them continued the northward line through Athenry to Tuam, both towns of some size, the latter also being a diocesan centre with a cathedral church. The two lines were the Athenry & Tuam (A&TR) and the Athenry & Ennis Junction (A&EJR) companies. The former was authorised by Act of Parliament in 1858 as a branch from the Midland Great Western's (MGWR) line from Dublin to Galway to link the two towns.   Athenry was an important station on the MGWR. This company viewed with concern any intrusions from other lines into what it regarded as its own rightful territory, and if possible it tried to exclude them. It undertook to work the A&TR, whose 15½ miles were built by William Dargan and opened in 1860. The agreement was that the MGWR should keep all the working receipts but pay a rent to the A&TR sufficient to allow a regular dividend of 3 per cent to be paid to the company's shareholders. In the agreement there was a provision that the A&TR should not promote or support any northward extension beyond Tuam, the fear being that traffic might be lost to it from the existing MGWR line from Athlone to Westport. The arrangement was satisfactory enough for the A&TR, since its dividends were thereby guaranteed, but less so for the working company since receipts from the line were falling. In 1870, therefore, the agreement was cancelled and the A&TR Directors decided to work the line themselves, in co-operation with the A&EJR.

The latter line had received Parliamentary sanction in 1859, but construction was delayed because of the prevailing trade depression. Work on it began in 1863, stopped for a while because there was no money to pay

Crusheen station looking towards Limerick, 7th June, 1961.   *H.C. Casserley*

The main station building and signal box at Crusheen, looking towards Athenry, 22nd September, 1955.   *R.M. Casserley*

'D17' class 4-4-0 No. 16 with the 9.00 am Galway to Limerick train takes water at Gort on 22nd April, 1955. *R.M. Casserley*

'D15' class 4-4-0 No. 298 is seen on the 7.00 am Limerick to Sligo train at Athenry on 30th June, 1938. *H.C. Casserley*

Athenry station looking towards Limerick on 21st April, 1955. The station nameboard reads 'Athenry & Ennis Junction'.   *H.C. Casserley*

Athenry station, view towards Sligo on the same day. The station nameboard at this end of the station reads 'Athenry & Tuam Junction'.   *H.C. Casserley*

'D15' class 4-4-0 No. 298 leaves Athenry on the 7.00 am Limerick to Sligo train on 30th June, 1938. This engine had been built as W&LR No. 55 *Bernard* in 1897.   *H.C. Casserley*

Ballyglunin station on 21st April, 1955, view towards Claremorris.   *H.C. Casserely*

Tuam on 20th April, 1955. The locomotive coaling facilities are visible on the left. Two'J15' class 0-6-0s can be seen, No. 187 on the turntable with No. 123 also in attendance.   *H.C. Casserley*

'D19' class 4-4-0 No. 45 stands at Tuam station with the 9.05 am Claremorris to Limerick train on 30th June, 1938.   *H.C. Casserley*

'D19' class 4-4-0 No. 6 stands outside the engine shed at Tuam on 30th June, 1938.
H.C. Casserley

Tuam station 17 years later than the view opposite with 'J15' class 0-6-0 No. 123 waiting to leave with the 3.10 pm to Galway on 21st April, 1955.
R.M. Casserley

the contractor, began again in the spring of 1865 and was broken off for a second time when the contractor went bankrupt. Eventually the company had to organise the completion of the line itself. Meanwhile the question, who was to work it, had to be settled. At first the W&LR, the obvious choice since it was already working the trains from Limerick to Ennis, was approached. Its Directors agreed, and the masterful William Malcomson, then the W&LR Chairman, was appointed as a Director. However, relations deteriorated between the two companies to the extent that unofficial soundings were made at M&GWR headquarters. The latter, however, declined to work the line; the W&LR got to know of these approaches and was not amused. So when the line was at last opened in 1869 its Board at first tried to work it themselves with borrowed locomotives and rolling stock. Three years later they realised that it was beyond their capabilities; there was nothing for it now but to eat humble pie and turn once more to the W&LR, which agreed to work it for a period of 20 years.

Just how unsatisfactory things had become before this happened is indicated by the events of November 1870. I quote from a short account of the line's history:

> In mid-November the Sheriff of Clare County seized the company's rolling stock in connection with some outstanding debts. There was a comical side to the affair. The Sheriff allowed the train to proceed with its passengers and freight in the custody of a set of bailiffs travelling on the engine. Four days later the train, complete with bailiffs, was seized by the County Galway Sheriff, who despatched the Clare bailiffs and refused to permit the train to proceed; the company had to hire cars to bring the passengers from Gort to Ennis. Kirwan (one of the line's Directors) made some arrangements with the Sheriff's office, and traffic resumed next day. However, in December a sale was advertised, of engines 1 and 2, which were the only assets of the company, the carriages and wagons being the property of Bristol Wagon Company, and engine No. 3 still owned by the Railway Rolling Stock Company. The sale took place, and the engines were bought by the railway's northern neighbour, the Athenry and Tuam, and they were in due course bought back, the price being made up by some moneys owed by the Tuam company for loco coal and the remainder discharged in instalments.*

By agreeing to work the A&EJR, and also the A&TR, the W&LR was greatly enlarging its empire - and at the same time incurring the animosity of the M&GWR, which opposed the scheme with every kind of legal obstruction it could think of. It was not so much the interloping W&LR that it feared; its Directors guessed - correctly, as it eventually turned out - that the GS&WR would eventually swallow it up, and between that line and itself there was little love to be lost. The M&GWR regarded the western parts of Ireland between Ennis and Sligo as peculiarly its own territory; let the GS&WR keep to its own south-western and southern regions and not muscle in on the areas belonging to its northern neighbour. For the W&LR to extend its influence to Tuam and perhaps beyond was one thing; for an enlarged GS&WR to do so was quite another. However, all the M&GW's machinations came to nought. The W&LR certainly wished to extend further north if it could; Sligo beckoned in the far distance, like Jerusalem to a crusading army. Almost at the end of the W&LR's

---

* *Journal of the Irish Railway Record Society*, Feb. 1990, article, Athenry to Ennis: W.E. Shepherd, p. 168.

corporate life it was to reach its goal. Whether it was worth it was another matter, for the line from Limerick to Sligo, passing through sparsely populated country, always remained a backwater.

However, further progress beyond Tuam was helped by two factors - a relatively generous British Government intent on 'killing Home Rule with kindness', and a line on the borders of Ulster whose Directors desired to tap the additional traffic that a line from Limerick might bring; this was the Sligo, Leitrim & Northern Counties Railway, whose Board had at first wished to build the line north from Tuam themselves and consented to the W&LR working it as a second-best. The first stage, to Claremorris on the M&GWR line from Athlone to Westport, was sanctioned by Parliament as early as 1872, but it lapsed, and permission had to be re-obtained in 1890. Construction began soon afterwards, and the new 17 mile stretch was opened at the end of 1894. The next extension, from Claremorris to Collooney Junction on the M&GWR line from Mullingar to Sligo, was begun at about the same time as the Tuam to Claremorris line, and finished in October 1895; construction was delayed through the contractor going bankrupt and another having to be found to complete what he had begun. It was this section which qualified for a free Government grant of as much as £146,000 towards its cost.

Great Southern Railways 'D14' class 4-4-0 No. 95 stands by with the 4.30 pm Sligo to Tuam train on 29th June, 1938.   *H.C. Casserley*

Claremorris station, looking south-east on 1st May, 1938 with the Midland Great Western Railway line to Athlone and Dublin curving to the left by the signal box and the Waterford, Limerick & Western line to Limerick curving to the right. On the far right, with its own platform is the branch to Ballinrobe, this line was closed in 1960.   *W.A. Camwell*

Claremorris station looking south on 29th June, 1938, the engine shed can be seen on the right.
H.C. Casserley

'J15' class 0-6-0 No. 229 pauses in front of the signal box at the northern end of Claremorris station during shunting duties on 20th April, 1955. *H.C. Casserley*

Claremorris station looking north on 7th June, 1961, showing the new platform and extended footbridge in the area formerly occupied by the engine shed. The rebuilding of the station commenced in 1942. *R.M. Casserley*

A large number of enthusiasts are in attendance to inspect the sorry state of Swinford station on 31st May, 1975, in this view looking towards Sligo.   *R.M. Casserley*

Tubbercurry station building as seen from the road on 1st June, 1975.   *R.M. Casserley*

Carrowmore station viewed from the train on 7th June, 1961. *H.C. Casserley*

'J15' class 0-6-0 No. 168 stands at Leyny station on a railtour in this scene looking towards Sligo on 1st June, 1975. *R.M. Casserley*

Waterford, Limerick & Western Railway trains continued their journey to Sligo over Midland Great Western Railway metals from Collooney Junction. This photograph at Ballysodare, looking south towards Mullingar, was taken on 29th June, 1938.   *H.C. Casserley*

'D19' class 4-4-0 No. 45 approaches Sligo with the 7.05 am from Tuam on 29th June, 1938.

H.C. Casserley

The locomotive crew of 'D14' class 4-4-0 No. 93 are seen applying strenuous effort in order to turn their locomotive on the turntable at Sligo on 18th May, 1950.   *H.C. Casserley*

The engine shed and turntable at Sligo on 29th June, 1938. The tracks to the passenger station lay to the left of the shed.   *H.C. Casserley*

The official seal of the Waterford, Limerick & Western Railway

To celebrate the achievement of its trains running through from Limerick to Sligo, in 1895 the W&LR renamed itself the Waterford, Limerick & Western Railway (WL&WR). From the point of view of route mileage over which its engines and rolling stock worked it was now the fourth largest railway in Ireland, and the only one in which it was not possible in a single day to travel between its remotest extremities.

The final position at Collooney Junction was that as the WL&WR line approached the MGWR line, under which it passed, a loop (WL&WR) ran up to North Junction on that line. Just after the bridge the WL&WR met the Sligo, Leitrim & Northern Counties Railway, from which a spur of that company ran northwards to join the MGWR. WL&WR trains passing over the M&GWR to Sligo had to carry a white board with a black star, or a red headlamp at night.

The end of the line for WL&WR trains was the MGWR terminus at Sligo. In this photograph taken on 29th June, 1938 'D17' class 4-4-0 No. 55 is in charge of the 9.10 am to Limerick.

H.C. Casserley

Chapter Seven

The Waterford, Limerick and Western Railway The Final Years of Independence

During 1895-1900 this line reached the height of its influence and importance. It had a route mileage of 350, over which its locomotives and rolling stock operated; of this, 32 miles was double-tracked, between Limerick and Limerick Junction and from Waterford to Fiddown; of this total mileage it owned slightly more than two-thirds. It could offer an end-to-end journey between its extreme limits, Waterford and Sligo, of 222 miles in its own rolling stock and behind its own locomotives; only the GS&WR could offer more, 235 miles from Dublin to Valentia Harbour, Europe's westernmost railhead. In point of time taken, the WL&WR exceeded its neighbour, for one could not travel from Waterford to Sligo in a single day by this route (though it could be done if one travelled by way of Kildare, Dublin and Mullingar on other lines). So there were presumably few through bookings by the WL&WR route from the one to the other.

Though the system was large it could not be termed prosperous. An examination of the published accounts shows this. While the Revenue Account was generally in credit balance, the Capital Account seldom was. Income and expenditure on this account, for the year beginning 1st July, 1898, was as set out in Appendix Three. Note particularly the debit balance of nearly £39,000, and the final two sentences beneath the Capital Account totals, which speak volumes. In the Revenue Account only a little over £1,000 remained each half-year to be carried over to the next half-year. This had been the general pattern over the previous decade. So far as its overall assets were concerned the railway was slowly bleeding to death. It seems surprising that in these circumstances it should have continued a policy of working other lines and taking them over when it could. No doubt its Directors hoped for the happy day when one of the acquired lines would turn out to be so profitable that it would provide reserves to set against the losses elsewhere.

It was able to keep going for two reasons. One was the interest that the United Kingdom Government was taking in Irish welfare, so that it put money into industrial and transport development in the poorer regions of Ireland in the hope of lessening discontent and the demand for Home Rule. The extension north of Claremorris was made possible by a Government grant. The other reason was the involvement of the GWR in England, which had expressed itself in money rebates each year so that the Irish line could pay dividends on its ordinary shareholders' stock. The line onwards from Waterford into Southern and Western Ireland was in a sense a continuation of the GWR's line through South Wales to Milford Haven. If it were not there, or fell into the hands of an unfriendly company, through traffic would be lost.

However, as explained in Chapter Four, the GWR Board towards the end of the century had been having second thoughts about this policy, and were planning a Fishguard-Rosslare route in place of the Milford-Waterford one and preparing to negotiate with the GS&WR regarding a shorter route to Cork which did not involve travel over the WL&WR line from Waterford to Limerick.

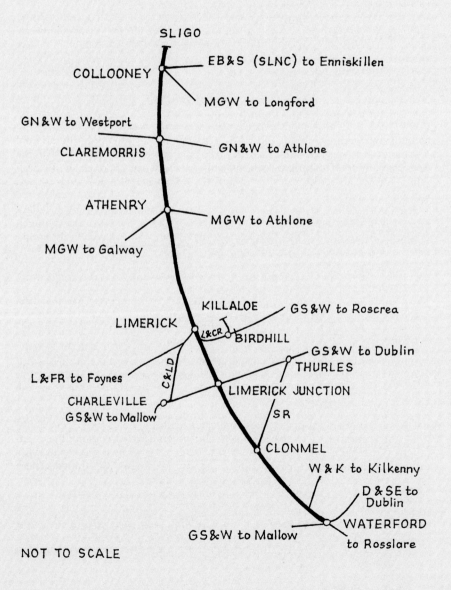

Faced with these possibilities and the threatened loss of the annual subsidy from Paddington, the WL&WR's Directors realised that their line had no independent future. There had always been divided counsels among them, between those who favoured the GWR connection and those who would have been glad for the GS&WR to take them over. On the part of the latter railway there was apprehension of what might happen to itself if an English company as strong and prestigious as the GWR muscled in on its territory and actually acquired the WL&WR. Negotiations began between the Boards of the two lines, the bargaining occurring chiefly in the area of what compensation should be paid to the WL&WR's shareholders, and it was finally agreed that the latter should be guaranteed 2½ per cent annually - which was a generous figure, as of late the WL&WR had not been paying as much as that on its ordinary stock.

On 1st January, 1901 the WL&WR ceased to exist, going out with the century. Its services were continued, first by the GS&WR, then after 1924 by the Great Southern (GSR), then by Coras Iompair Eireann (CIE), and since 1987 by Iarnrod Eireann. Passenger use of the line and its branches diminished, many of the latter were eventually closed to passengers, and now only the original line between Waterford and Limerick has passenger services, together with the line from Limerick to Ennis and the short length between Limerick and Birdhill which forms part of the alternative route from Limerick to Dublin via Nenagh and Ballybrophy.

The extent of traffic on the line during its final five years of independent existence is reflected in the working timetable for October 1895, a copy of which is held in the archives of the National Library of Ireland. It shows the following pattern of trains daily between Waterford and Limerick:

Three passenger trains stopping at all or most stations to Limerick and taking between 3 and 3½ hours.
Two goods trains, running at night or during the early morning, calling at all or most stations and taking about 6½ hours.
One mixed train as far as Tipperary, continuing to Limerick with passengers only, taking 3½ hours.
One evening mixed train, which also conveyed the mails, taking 4 hours and 20 minutes. On Sunday evenings, one mixed and one goods train took 4 hours and 20 minutes and 6¾ hours respectively.
An afternoon goods train also ran from Tipperary to Limerick taking 1 hour and 50 minutes, on both weekdays and Sundays.

The company's through services connected with the boats to or from South Wales at Waterford. The same vessels and others carried commodities. An article in the December 1900 issue of the *Railway Magazine* by the WL&WR's district superintendent, Mr W. Beddoes, details the commodities traded. There was a considerable traffic in cattle, sheep and pigs, transported alive from Waterford and slaughtered on arrival at their destinations. There was also a considerable export of poultry and game, fish, dairy products and eggs. One speciality was salmon, netted in the lower reaches of the Shannon and Suir and dispatched to grace the tables of well-to-do Londoners, together with lobsters, crabs and oysters, while for the lower orders there were eels and winkles,

Code of Engine Whistling Signals.

All Stations other than Junctions, - -	1 Whistle
Limerick—To or from Ennis Line, - -	3 Whistles
Do. Foynes and Kerry Line Trains to and from Station and Check Platform,	2 ,,
Do. To or from Cork Direct— Junction Signals :—	
W. & L. Ry. Trains -	,,
G. S. & W. ,, -	- ,,
Do. To or from Engine House Lines,	4 short
Killonan Junc.—To and from Killaloe Branch	2 Whistles
*Limerick Junc.—Approaching from Limerick	3 ,,
Do. ,, ,, Waterford	2 ,,
Clonmel Junc.—To and from—Thurles Branch	2 ,,
Thurles Junc.— ,, ..	3 ,,
Waterford— ,, Engine House Lines	1 long and 1 short Whistle
Do. Junc. To and from (W. & L. Ry. Passenger Trains - - -	2 Whistles
Do. Junc. ,, (,, Cattle Trains)	1 ,,
Do. Junc. ,, (W. C. I. Ry. Trains)	3 ,,
Do. Passenger Station—To and from	1 ,,
Do. North Wharf Junc.—To and from	3 ,,
†Athenry Junc.—Approaching from Tuam -	2 ,,
Do. ,, ,, Ennis -	3 ,,
Claremorris Station.	
From or to Ballyhaunis, - - - -	1 long ,,
,, ,, Balla, - - -	2 ,, ,,
,, ,, Tuam (W. & L.) - -	3 ,, ,,
,, ,, Sligo (W. & L.) - -	4 ,, ,,
,, ,, Ballinrobe, - - -	1 ,, 1 short
Loop for Up Line, - - - -	2 ,, 1 ,,
,, ,, Down - - - -	2 ,, 2 ,,
Down Line to Up Line, and vice versa - -	2 ,,
Through Cross-Over Down Line to Goods Siding (Ground frame) - -	3 ,,
Up Loop to Goods Siding (Ground frame) -	1 ,, 2 ,,
Sligo—From Ballysodare to Passenger Station -	1 ,, Whistle
,, ,, Goods ,,	3 ,, ,,
To Ballysodare from Passenger ,, -	1 ,, ,,
,, ,, Goods ,, -	3 ,, ,,
From or to Engine Shed Sidings -	2 ,,
Backing out of Passenger Station -	1 & 2 short ,,
Crossing from Down to Up Line or vice versa -	2 short
Ballysodare—To or from Carrignagat Junction —M. G. W.	1 long Whistle
,, —W & L.	2 ,, ,,
,, —S. L. & N. C.	3 ,, ,,
Carrignagat—From or to M. G. W. (Main Line)	1 ,, ,,
,, ,, S. L. & N. C. (Branch)	3 ,, ,,
,, ,, W. & L. (Branch)	2 ,, ,,
Collooney Junction—From or to Collooney —M. G. W.	1 long 1 short
From or to Collooney —W. & L.	1 ,, 2 ,,
Patrick's Well Junc.—To and from W. & L. Ry. Trains	1 whistle
Do. To and from G. S. & W. Trains	2 ,,
Ballingrane Junc.—To and from Newcastle -	1 ,,
,, Foynes Branch -	2 ,,
Newcastle Junc.—To and from Limerick -	1 ,,
Do. ,, Tralee -	2 ,,
Tralee and Fenit -	2 ,,

N.B.—See Great Southern and Western Rules

See Midland Great Western Rules.

The elaborate whistling code for locomotive drivers in use in November 1895, surely most difficult to remember.

National Library of Irealnd, Dublin

LOADS OF GOODS TRAINS.

Station-Masters, Inspectors, Guards, Enginemen, Shunters and others are instructed that the loading of the Goods Trains must be regulated as below ; but in urgent cases Enginemen and Guards are not strictly confined to this list to the extent of a few Vehicles. In exceptionally bad weather the Drivers are not restricted to the undermentioned Loads : they must take what they can after consultation with the Station-Master and Guard.

ENGINES NUMBER.	Waterford to Limerick.	Limerick to Waterford.	Clonmel to Thurles.	Thurles to Clonmel.	Limerick to Killaloe.	Killaloe to Limerick.	Limerick to Ennis.	Ennis to Limerick.	Ennis to Athenry.	Athenry to Ennis.	Athenry to Tuam.	Tuam to Athenry.	Limerick to Newcastle.	Newcastle to Limerick.	Newcastle to Barnagh.	Barnagh to Tralee.	Tralee to Barnagh.
24, 40, 41, 45, 46, 49, 50	45	45	35	40	45	40	40	40	35	35	40	40	40	40	20	40	25
1, 5, 6, 7	35	40	30	35	40	35	35	35	30	30	35	35	35	35	18	38	20
9, 12, 19, 26, 27, 33	30	35	25	30	35	30	30	30	25	25	30	30	28	28	14	30	18
10, 20, 22, 23, 43, 44, 47, 48	25	30	25	30	30	30	30	30	25	25	25	25	25	25	12	25	14
3, 8, 13, 14, 15, 25, 30, 31, 32, 35, 36, 37, 38, 39, 51, 52	20	25	20	25	30	25	25	25	25	25	25	25	25	25	12	25	14
2, 4, 11, 16, 17, 18, 21	18	22	15	20	20	18	20	20	20	20	20	20	20	20	9	15	12
28	...	...	...	...	...	...	...	...	...	...	...	...	...	...	...	...	...

Under and Overloading to be immediately reported to the Traffic Manager and Locomotive Superintendent.

When Wagons are loaded with Coal, Corn, Flour, or similar dead weight, 5 Vehicles to be deducted from loads given.

Empty Wagons to be classified and considered thus—3 empties equal 2 loaded.

Engines to be assisted up Waterford and Clonmel Banks (including Southern Branch) when application is made for Bank Engine.

If an Engineman refuses to take on Trucks from any Station, it will be the duty of the Station-Master, or person in authority to endorse upon his (the Engineman's) Train-Ticket the fact of his having done so, and report to Traffic Manager.

Wagons on Passenger and Mixed Trains to be coupled by Screw Couplings.

Left: Permitted loadings in goods vehicles for different locomotives: from Working timetable for November 1895.
National Library of Ireland Dublin

Below: Newly-built Robinson 4-4-0 No. 55 *Bernard* heading a specially prepared train for conveying the Duke and Duchess of York on 31st August, 1897. The second and fourth coaches are bogie lavatory composites and the third vehicle is the Directors' saloon; they are standing outside the Limerick carriage shop.

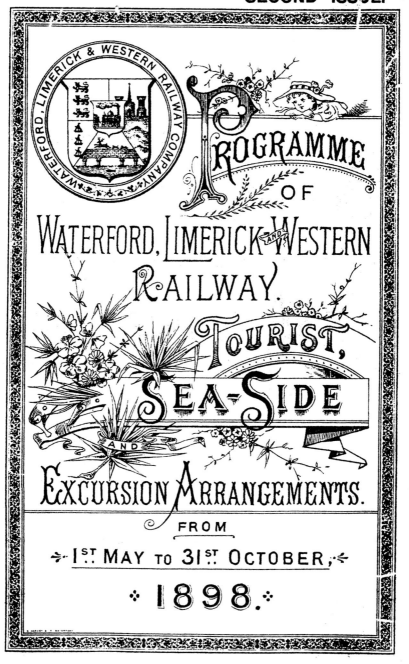

The cover of a Public Notice regarding special tourist arrangements on the WL&WR during the summer and autumn of 1898. Note the typical Victorian decoration with an admixture of sentiment! *National Library of Ireand, Dublin*

together with snared rabbits.   Hams and bacon, cured at Limerick and Waterford, were also exported in large amounts.   In the chief towns along the line there were factories producing condensed milk, while Clonmel and Limerick also made margarine.   Among non-foodstuffs one interesting item of export was uniform clothing for the British Army produced at a Limerick factory which employed as many as 800 hands, mostly young women.   In the opposite direction there was a traffic in coal from the pits in South Wales - a necessary import since Ireland has hardly any coal of its own, and no way was then known of using the turves from its peat bogs except for burning in domestic fireplaces.

As to goods carried though not exported, timber may be mentioned, though not much tree-felling was carried out in Ireland in those days; more important to the native Irishman was the traffic in whisky and beer; Limerick had a large distillery and Clonmel a brewery.   Killaloe had quarries producing stone and slate of good quality, much of which was carried away on the railway.

Although the tourist potential of Southern Ireland was not yet being fully exploited, the country's natural charms were beginning to be recognised, and English visitors were already being attracted to resorts along the west coast and among the western mountains, particularly after royal personages had begun to patronise them.   Anglers in particular were attracted, for Ireland offered trout and salmon fishing which, so far as the latter was concerned, the south-country Englishman would have had to go to Scotland for.

Finally, one has to mention the horse, an animal which in Ireland receives almost religious devotion.   Those who have read the novels and short stories of Somerville and Ross, so popular in Edwardian days, will appreciate how much horses and hunting matter in rural Ireland.   Irish bloodstock was exported to England, to hunting and racing stables, where their qualities were appreciated as if they had been bred in Arabia.   At horse fairs in the principal centres, particularly Limerick, Rathkeale, Clonmel, Thurles, Ennis, Athenry and Tuam, buyers from all parts of the United Kingdom came to inspect the animals on offer.

Thus, on the eve of its disappearance as an independent company, the WL&WR showed a confident and, to all appearances, prosperous face to the world. It ran no expresses, but its carriages were comfortable, its stations well built and in some cases impressive, and in its last years its trains were hauled by some of the handsomest locomotives to be found on any Irish railway. It had an excellent record of freedom from fatal accidents   In the words of Shakespeare, 'Tis not in mortals to command success, But we'll do more - deserve it'.   The Waterford, Limerick & Western certainly deserved it. However, after it had lost its principal backer, the English GWR, it could only sell itself to its rival, the GS&WR, as dearly as possible and vanish gracefully from the scene.

Waterford to Limerick and environs.

Reproduced by kind permission of Bartholomew's Maps

Chapter Eight

The Course of the Line and the Main Line Stations

The line will be described going from east to west, as it is found at present, changes from W&LR days being noted in passing. The second part of the chapter describes the main line stations in more detail.

Waterford station, the terminus of the railway since 1864, is situated on the north bank of the Suir at the foot of a steep cliff locally known as 'Mount Misery' and at the northern end of the bridge leading to the town itself. All trains now run from the north face of the long single platform.

From the station the line heads westwards, keeping close to the Suir for rather less than a mile and then veering away from it to the north-west; at this point the line divides, at Newrath Junction, the right fork going to Kilkenny and Dublin. This was formerly the Waterford and Kilkenny Railway, with which the W&LR had such a bad relationship in earlier days, and which for a few years it worked. Dunkitt station, at the junction, was closed in 1855. The left fork, the former W&LR, now bears west again, rising fairly steeply at 1 in 100/150 to milepost 73¼, undulating as far as the site of the former Grange station (of which the level crossing gates now remain) and then falling again to approach the left bank of the Suir just beyond Fiddown. Fiddown was formerly the station that served the small town of Portlaw, three miles away to the south across the river; here, too, the station has gone but the crossing gates remain. To this point the line was formerly double tracked but was later singled. Two miles beyond Fiddown, on the left-hand side of the line, glimpses may occasionally be had of the Comeragh Mountains whose main ridge, extending from south-east to north-west, culminates in a peak a little under 2,600 feet high, beneath whose eastward-facing crags are some of the best rock climbs in Ireland.

Carrick-on-Suir, 14¼ miles from Waterford, is reached at a two-platform station with a crossing loop a quarter of a mile short of the town centre. Here, as mentioned in Chapter One, the first Limerick-Waterford line to be proposed was to terminate, since Carrick was the furthest point upstream on the Suir to which barges could be brought from Waterford. It is a pleasant market town of some 5,000 inhabitants and boasts a well-preserved Elizabethan fortified mansion, Carrick Castle, open to view by visitors.

Beyond Carrick the line continues with a rising tendency as far as Kilsheelan, where there was a station in W&LR days. Beyond here the rising gradients become more pronounced as the railway leaves the river and main road and curves away from the Suir, crossing two minor summits before falling to Clonmel, where the station is over half a mile from the town centre. Just short of the station the line from Thurles formerly came in on the right; it has now been dismantled. Clonmel, the chief town of County Tipperary, with about 14,500 inhabitants, is a market centre with some light industry; it has some fine modern churches and a garrison fort built by Cromwell. It also has literary links with the past; Lawrence Sterne was born here in 1714 and the novelist Anthony Trollope worked for a while at the post office in his younger days.

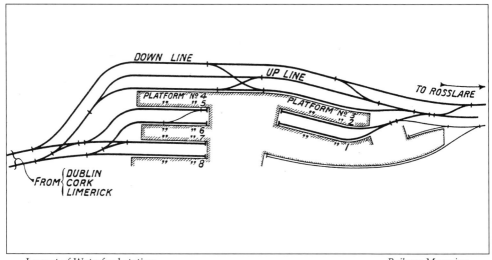

Layout of Waterford station.   *Railway Magazine*

'J15' class 0-6-0 No. 241 approaches Waterford from the west on 2nd July, 1938. *H.C. Casserley*

A view along platforms 3 and 4 at Waterford on 12th April, 1955. Note the crossing which separates the two platforms (*see plan opposite*). *H.C. Casserley*

'J15' class 0-6-0 No. 157 is seen at the western end of Waterford station on 12th April, 1955. *R.M. Casserley*

The WL&WR shed at Waterford. The engine shed is on the site of the original Newrath terminus of 1854.   *Real Photographs*

No. 461 stands below the gantry-mounted signal box at the western end of Waterford station on 6th June, 1961.   *R.M. Casserley*

The approach to Waterford from Limerick on 18th June, 1939, looking east, with the River Suir on the right and the bridge linking the station with the city in the distance.

R.W. Miller Collection

The Waterford coal stage and turntable alongside the jetty on the River Suir on 18th June, 1939. The ship is the SS *Carrickmore* built in Aberdeen in 1925.   *R.W. Miller Collection*

Grange station looking towards Waterford on 12th April, 1955. This was one of the least used stations on the main line.   *H.C. Casserley*

Fiddown station looking towards Waterford on 12th April, 1955 with 'J15' class 0-6-0 No. 166 at the platform.   *H.C. Casserley*

Carrick-on-Suir station seen from the window in an eastbound train as it passes from the loop onto the single track on 15th July, 1972.   *Author*

Carrick-on-Suir station from the train looking towards Limerick on 12th April, 1955.
                                                                                                    H.C. Casserley

Clonmel station buildings from the road on 7th June, 1964. *R.M. Cassserley*

A 1992 photograph of the solid Victorian stonework of Clonmel in which limestone was used.
  Author

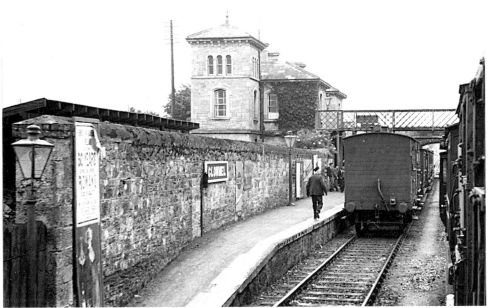

A busy scene at Clonmel looking towards Limerick on 2nd July, 1938.   *H.C. Casserley*

'J15' class 0-6-0 No. 171 arrives at Clonmel with the 10.15 am Waterford to Limerick train on 2nd July, 1938.   *H.C. Casserley*

'D10' class 4-4-0 No. 313 at Clonmel engine shed on 2nd July, 1938.   *H.C. Casserley*

A view looking east at Clonmel on 18th June, 1939 showing the engine shed and the branch to Thurles curving round the back to head north past the distant Slievenamon (2,368 ft).
R.W. Miller Collection

After Clonmel the line leaves the Suir valley, since at this point the river makes a circuitous bend to the south. Still heading westwards, it climbs steeply, mostly at 1 in 132, to a summit at milepost 43¼, the second highest point on the line. At and beyond this point, as the line makes a wide curve towards the north, a splendid view of the Comeragh, Knockmealdown and Galtee mountain ranges opens up on the left. Some connoisseurs of Irish scenery reckon that this is the finest prospect to be enjoyed anywhere in Ireland from the windows of a railway carriage. The Knockmealdowns top 2,600 feet at their highest point, while Galtee More at 3,018 feet is the fourth highest summit in Ireland. A little further on Cahir is reached, a little town of about 2,000 inhabitants, whose principal attraction is a splendid castle, dating mainly from the 15th century, built on the site of an Iron Age fort. Beyond Cahir station, which formerly had a passing loop which has now been removed, the line crosses the Suir by an impressive girder bridge, the scene in 1955 of the very unusual accident described in Appendix Four.

The line now leaves the Suir valley, passes through a defile flanked by two high cliffs, known locally as the 'Khyber Pass', curves to the west around the eastern end of the Galtee range and crosses the entrance to the Glen of Aherlow, the scene of many ancient battles and retreat of many outlaws. At Cappagh level crossing can be seen old gravel pits, from which in W&LR days hundreds of tons of gravel were taken to ballast the line. Steadily rising, the line passes the site of the former station at Bansha, which could have been used very infrequently since it served only a small village. Circumventing the end of the range of low hills which close in the Glen of Aherlow to the north, the line makes westwards to the town of Tipperary, where the station building lies just to the south of the town. Tipperary has just under 5,000 inhabitants; it has no special features of attraction. The famous World War I song suggests that it was specially noted for the beauty of its young women, and that may still be so, though at the time of the author's visit they must mostly have been indoors.

From Tipperary the line turns north, then north-west, and reaches its summit at milepost 22¾; here one passes the watershed between the Suir and Shannon basins. Two miles further Kean's Points are reached, where the train has first to back down the spur through Limerick Junction and then run forward into the western bay platform of that station - the only place in Ireland where the layout requires a double reversal before the platform can be reached. The above-named points preserve the name of the original pointsman, who with his two daughters operated the mechanism for many years. There was no signal box so he or they had to be out in all weathers and by night as well as by day. (It is recorded that Kean was bold enough to ask for a cloak for each of his two daughters, and to his surprise received them.)

Having left Limerick Junction by means of a single reversal, the train proceeds to Limerick itself on a 22-miles' downhill journey. There are now no intermediate stations, but in W&LR days there were five - Oola, Pallas, Dromkeen, Boher and Killonan. Pallas station buildings are still there; the others were not noticed on the author's own journey down the line. The railway keeps to the southern side of a widening pastoral valley, with low hills to the left and higher ones to the right, the Slievefelim mountains beyond which the Shannon flows to its estuary. In W&LR days there was double track right through to Limerick, which has for some while now been singled. Along this stretch the GS&WR had running powers into

Cahir station seen from the road on 7th June, 1964.   *T.J. Edgington*

The disused platform at Cahir in 1992, inaccessible to the public but still kept neat and trim, with paintwork and tubs of flowers, perhaps in hope of increased passenger traffic that will justify the replacement of the loop.   *Author*

The main platform at Cahir station in July 1993.   *Author*

Diesel-electric locomotive No. 036 on a westbound train of oil wagons passing through Cahir in July 1993. As the passing loop has been removed the stairs to the footbridge have been closed with gates. This leaves a 25 mile block section now between Clonmel and Tipperary.   *Author*

Limerick, and at the present day through trains from Dublin can run through without having to stop at Limerick Junction, by means of a recently-built spur.

At Killonan the line from Ballybrophy, Roscrea and Nenagh comes in on the right, and a little further on the line from Ennis and Sligo joins it also. The spires and towers of Limerick are now in view. A little later the line from Foynes comes in on the left, still in use for freight though no longer offering a passenger service. Finally one enters the terminus.

The Main Stations Described

There were two terminal and 14 intermediate stations along the main route of the W&LR during its years of independent existence; there are now (2000) only five intermediate stations - Carrick-on-Suir, Clonmel, Cahir, Tipperary and Limerick Junction. This section deals with them as they now observably are, and only by reference or incidental allusion to them as they used to be. Those that have been closed and whose structures have been demolished or turned to other uses are not of much interest now and photographs are difficult to obtain; however, it has been possible to get some information from the Ordnance Survey of 1908, when there was a 25 in./mile coverage of inhabited areas, and portions of the appropriate map are shown on adjacent pages.

Waterford itself, as befits the fifth largest population centre in the Republic, has a fine station, rather unusually arranged, which has altered considerably since it was first built. Right up to the end of the company's independent existence it was a terminus, the road frontage then facing to the east, but with the building of lines eastwards from it to Wexford and Rosslare after the GS&WR had taken the company over in 1901 alterations were made. A bay platform was added in 1904, and a whole new through station opened on 30th August, 1906, though the old station did not close until 31st January, 1908. It now has a single long platform face at which all trains draw up or from which they leave; former platform bays at either end are now only used for shunting. This platform is glass-canopied for the greater part of its length. Access from outside is now gained through doors on the station building's southern face, opposite the north end of the main bridge across the Suir. Behind and within them is the booking office; to the right of it is a buffet selling excellent food; to the left are the doors on to the platform, which are opened only a short while after a train has arrived and before one is due to depart. North of the line through the main platform are through lines which allow freight trains to by-pass the station; immediately beyond them is the steep cliff-side of 'Mount Misery'. Over the central part of the platform, behind the offices and buffet, the roof has been lowered and covered in with wooden planking in which neon lights are fixed; the platform surface at this point is covered with large tiles, alternately black and white like a chessboard; the rest is paved with stone. A large overhead signal box straddles the platform and goods lines at the west end; no doubt it will eventually be disused when semaphore gives place to colour-light signalling, but one hopes that the box will be preserved as it is unique in its placing and apparently in good condition still. The 1906 bridge over the Suir measured 1,205 ft, with six spans of 140 ft, one of 103 ft, and an opening span of 50 ft.

Most trains which now leave Waterford head for Dublin, from whence most incoming trains arrive. They leave the former W&LR main line a little to the west of the station and curve northwards for Kilkenny (where all reverse), Kildare and Dublin. Those using the former W&LR metals are reduced now to two each way in the summer and one in the winter and are through from and to Rosslare to and from Limerick. They form only a small part of the traffic along this route; there is (as related in a later chapter) a good deal more freight traffic now than passenger traffic.

The next station going westwards was Grange, which had two platforms but was not remarkable in any way. Fiddown, the one after it, was, if not remarkable, in one respect unique. As soon as the line had reached this point in 1853, one important regular user, William Malcomson, Chairman of the line from 1860 to 1871, whose private residence was at Portlaw, three miles from the station, ordained the building beside the latter of a private toilet, for himself and family and no one else unless he authorised it. There were of course no toilets on the trains, and waiting could no doubt be uncomfortable. The station master held the key and opened it when instructed. One cannot well imagine a more unusual example of the exercise of a *droit de seigneur*. The building is still there. At Fiddown the double track from Waterford ceased and the line was single the rest of the way to Limerick Junction.

At Carrick-on-Suir there is a passing place and two platforms with an overbridge of a type standard elsewhere on the line, there is also a goods bay at the western end. The main station building is on the southern side of the loop, a low one-storey affair. All passenger trains now use this platform. Kilsheelan station, like Grange, was a small affair and has now vanished. Clonmel, on the other hand, boasts a really massive stone-built station, as befits the largest town in Tipperary County and the third largest on the line; from here the railway to Thurles formerly ran. The main building is large, substantially built of grey stone; its waiting room now serves not only for rail passengers but also for those travelling by bus, as all road public transport calls at the station forecourt. Clonmel, like Carrick, was and is a passing place with two platforms; passenger trains normally use the southern platform. As at Carrick, too, a handsome iron footbridge connects the two sides of the station. The north platform is shut in by a well-built stone wall several feet high, now becoming somewhat overgrown with greenery in places. The station frontage shows a two-storey building with a small tower at the eastern end and three massive chimney stacks. Immediately to the east is a very large warehouse with an arched roof of corrugated iron and glass, one of the biggest structures on the line.

Continuing to Cahir, one finds another unique structure, for the station building was not constructed as such, but was formerly a hunting lodge of the Earls of Glengall, which was sold to the railway, who adapted it suitably. With steep roofs, windows with shallow-pointed lintels and diamond-shaped panes, and crowned by two enormous chimneys (one of which now anachronistically bears a television aerial for the benefit of the station master's family) it still resembles what it once was when seen from the forecourt. The hunting stables have now been adapted for use as a depot by the Irish telecommunications service. Going through the front door, one confronts a wrought iron staircase, which one ascends to reach the platform, which is about 15 ft above the level of the road outside. The station itself has the usual lattice-work overbridge, but passengers cannot use it since on both platforms it is shut off by a locked gate.

Tipperary station.

Reproduced from the 25″, 1904 Ordnance Survey Map

This does not matter since there is now only one track through the station, the one beside the former north platform having been lifted after the fatal accident to a freight train in 1955, referred to in Appendix Four. However - a nice Irish touch! - the platform is still kept as if regularly used; there are posters on the boards in the shelter which would be legible to anyone with a pair of binoculars, and the shelter-lintel bears the station's name in Irish characters; flowers grow in tubs along the platform. Recently, outside any passenger train-arrival time, the author was surprised to hear the noise of one approaching; a few seconds later a diesel locomotive hurried through at about 50 mph at the head of a train of oil wagons - a reminder that there is much freight movement on the line still.

The next station, at Bansha, has gone, and Tipperary is now the last stopping place before Limerick Junction. Here it is the platform on the north-eastern side which is used by passengers; beside it is a massive stone station building with bay windows jutting out on to the platform and a shallow-pitched slate roof. From the forecourt the station displays an almost Mediterranean appearance, belied by the weather on the day when the author photographed it; it is two storeys high. The footbridge does not link the two platforms but crosses the line to the south-east of a road level crossing, so is probably more used by non-passengers than by those taking the train, who in any case alight only at the north-eastern side platform now. A massive stone wall along the edge of this platform is lined with flower beds. Tipperary is the highest wayside station on the line; a mile and-a half beyond it the gradients begin to fall towards Limerick.

Limerick Junction was three miles further on. Though it was built to serve through trains between Dublin and Cork in either direction and give connections to Limerick for their passengers, it needs special mention because W&LR trains used it, and still do, in a very unusual manner. The W&LR line

GSR 0-6-0s, 'J15' class No. 106 and 'J25' class No. 239, are seen entering Tipperary station with a westbound passenger train on 30th June, 1938.   *H.C. Casserley*

A general view of Tipperary station looking towards Limerick on 22nd April, 1955.

R.M. Casserley

A view along the platform at Tiperrary station on 2nd July, 1938.   *H.C. Casserley*

The station frontage and forecourt at Tipperary in July 1993. *Author*

Looking towards Waterford at Limerick Junction on 22nd June, 1939 showing the level crossing between the single track W&L and the double track GS&WR. *R.W. Miller Collection*

Limerick Junction

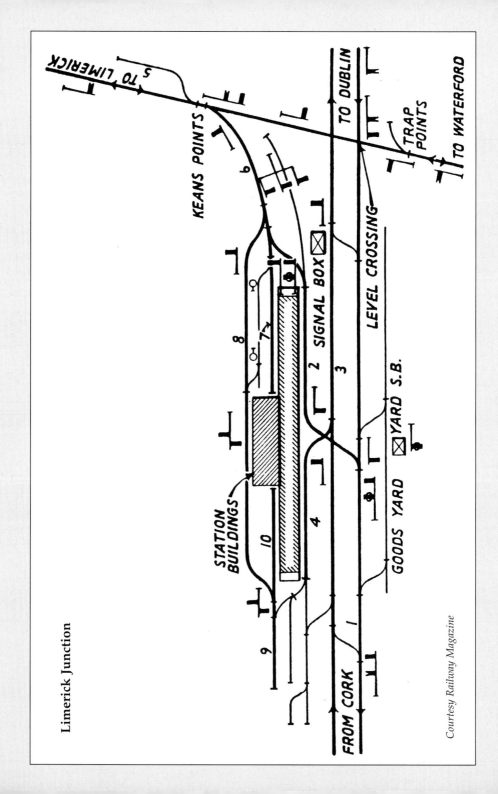

Courtesy Railway Magazine

The level crossing at Limerick Junction looking north towards Limerick. The double track main line runs east to Dublin and west to Cork.   *H.C. Casserley*

crosses the former G&SWR main line obliquely on the level; a little further on are Kean's Points which make a trailing connection coming in from Limerick Junction, whose layout is shown, diagrammatically, on page 100. Trains from Dublin came into platform 2 prior to 1967 after stopping and reversing back; those from Cork similarly stopped and reversed back into platform 3. Trains from Limerick terminating at the Junction ran into platform 1, the locomotive then running round the train to haul it back to Limerick again. All this was complicated and time-wasting enough, and the movements of main line trains have now been simplified by the addition of facing points so that trains from either direction can run into either platform 2 or platform 3 and regain their proper metals without having to reverse. It is otherwise with trains from Limerick to Waterford, which have to diverge to the right at Kean's Points, run round behind the station and across a level crossing over the station approach road, proceed into a siding and then reverse back into platform 4. When leaving again two reversals were necessary, one out of the siding, backing to a point beyond Kean's Points, and then going forward again, crossing the former GS&WR line on the level and so proceeding to Waterford. Something similar occurred with trains from the Waterford direction. All these manoeuvres took up, and take up, a good deal of time.

Limerick Junction stands on its own in open countryside and is mostly an exchange point. Its single platform has been greatly lengthened in the Dublin

Kean's Points at Limerick Junction, looking towards Limerick on 22nd June, 1939. The curve from Limerick Junction station can just be made out approaching from the left.

R.W. Miller Collection

The W&L side of Limerick Junction in 1933. Limerick bound trains used the platform in the mid-distance. The track in the foreground leads to the platform used by the trains to Waterford.

L&GRP

'D12' class 4-4-0 No. 306 stands at the platform (*right*) at Limerick Junction awaiting departure for Limerick on 23rd April, 1955. *R.M. Casserley*

4-4-0 No. 23 is seen shunting a dining car at Limerick Junction in 1933. *L&GRP*

A view along the platform at Limerick Junction in 1933. The line to Limerick can be just distinguished as it curves away to the left.   *L&GRP*

Limerick Junction on 30th June, 1938 looking towards Dublin. 'J15' class 0-6-0 No. 118 is busy shunting while the Limerick platform is on the left.   *H.C. Casserley*

Limerick Junction looking south-west, with the GS&WR main line from Dublin on the left behind the North signal box, and the W&LR curve from Kean's Points on the right. The 5.35 pm train from Limerick on 22nd June, 1939 has called at Limerick Junction platform and is now being propelled back round the curve before resuming its journey to Waterford.

R.W. Miller Collection

'K1' class 2-6-0 No. 384 is seen in the west bay platform at Limerick Junction with a Waterford train on 30th June, 1938.

H.C. Casserley

'D14' class 4-4-0 No. 64 approaches Limerick Junction with the 5.50 from Limerick to Waterford on 30th June, 1938. The engine shed can be seen on the right.   *H.C. Casserley*

'D11' class 4-4-0 No. 304 is seen outside the engine shed at Limerick Junction on 23rd April, 1955.
H.C. Casserley

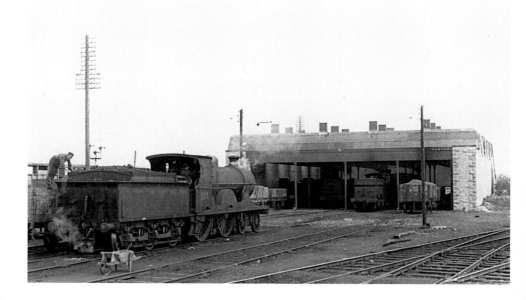

The central crossing at Limerick Junction in July 1992. The structure in the centre, middle distance is the stone-built water tower used in steam days.   *Author*

Limerick Junction station, July 1992: the cross-over in the middle of what was formerly a uniquely complicated layout, when all main line trains between Dublin and Cork in both directions had to stop away from the platform and then set back into it. This has now been obviated by the installation of additional points.   *Author*

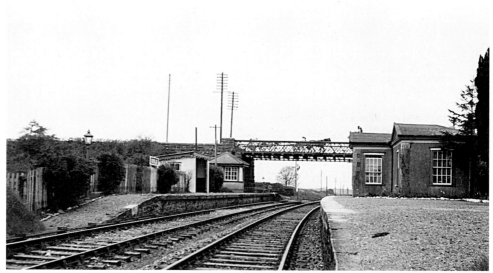

Oola station looking towards Limerick on 23rd April, 1955.   *R.M. Casserley*

A view from the overbridge of Oola station looking towards Waterford on 23rd April, 1955.
H.C. Casserley

Dromkeen station as seen from the train.   *H.C. Casserley*

direction so that full-length trains can pull up at platform 2 short of the crossing point.   The adjacent photographs give some impression of the station's appearance and of the main platform's great length.

There are now no intermediate stopping places between the Junction and Limerick. Of the former stations, Oola, Pallas, Pallas, Dromkeen, Boher and Killonan, only two still have anything to show for themselves - Pallas, where the remains of the platform shelter still survive, and Killonan, where the main building was so large as to resemble a public meeting hall faced with Greek columns. In its spacious main room, in the days of the line's independence, Directors gathered for Board meetings. The building is now in private hands but the owner takes a pride in its upkeep.

Limerick station itself, a little under half a mile from the City centre, is a terminal whose exterior faces a large concourse which now serves as a car park. Its architecture has been criticised as heavy and uninteresting; the author found it dignified even though it lacks any Grecian graces. Behind the facade is a wide concourse giving access to two platform structures, each with two faces, the southernmost of which has been greatly extended after the removal of the sharp rightward branch to Foynes and Tralee. The platforms are numbered from the left as one faces their entrances, and only 1, 2 and 3 are regularly used. There is a buffet to the right of the concourse. The station has a large all-over roof with

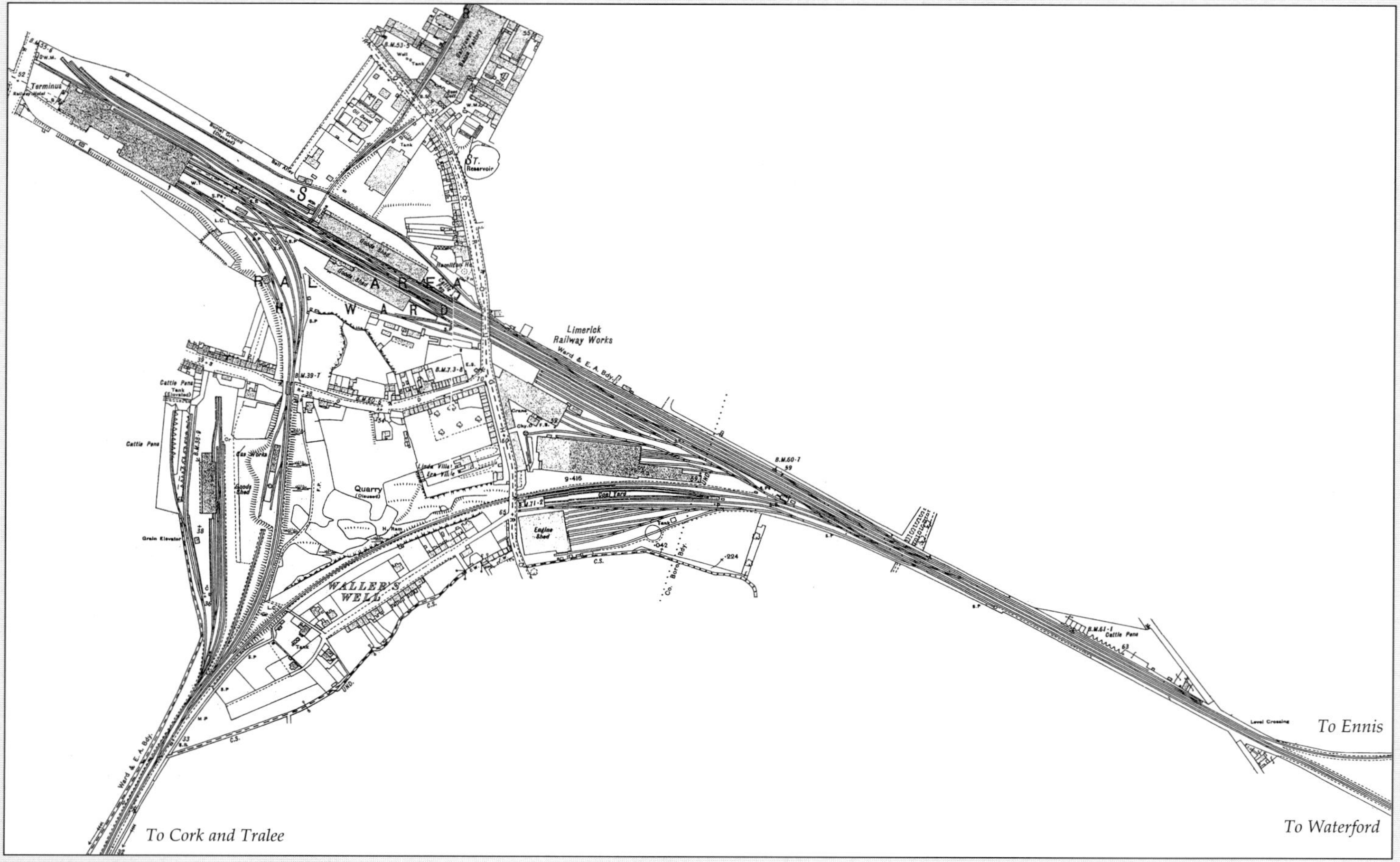

Limerick station.

To Ennis

To Waterford

To Cork and Tralee

Limerick Railway Works

Quarry

WALLER'S WELL

An undated view of Limerick station. The line to Waterford curves to the right, while those curving away to the left are for Tralee. *Real Photographs*

Limerick station on 16th April, 1955. *R.M. Casserley*

A fine selection of starting signals at Limerick's platform ends greet a Robinson 2-4-0 arriving with a train from Waterford in 1929.   *L&GRP*

'J15' class 0-6-0 No. 125 prepares to leave Limerick on 7th June, 1961.   *T.J. Edgington*

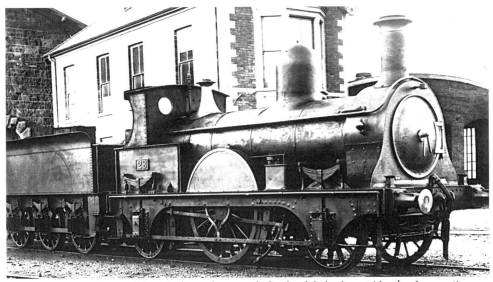

Kitson 2-2-2 of 1864 No. 28, formerly named *South of Ireland*, outside the Locomotive Superintendent's office at Limerick, at various times occupied by such well-known engineers as Martin Atock, Henry Appleby and John Robinson. Part of the engine shed can be seen on the extreme right *c*. 1895.   *L&GRP*

Inside the locomotive erecting shop at Limerick Works on 18th June, 1939. The engines under repair are left: 'F6' class 2-4-2T No. 42 (normally the Birr branch engine), centre rear: 'J15' class 0-6-0 No. 174, right: 'D19' class 4-4-0 No. 45.   *R.W. Miller Collection*

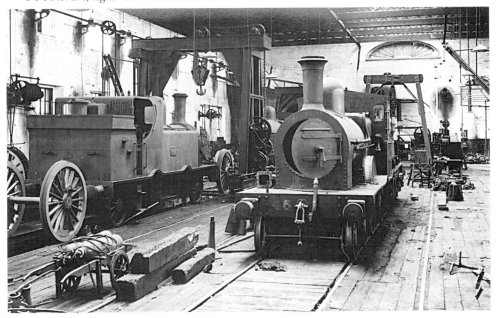

Bo-Bo No. 185 is seen beneath the train shed at Limerick in July 1993.   *Author*

A view along the platform at Limerick looking towards Limerick Junction in July 1993. In the distance the large overbridge which crossed the former W&LR line near where the line to Birdhill curved away can be seen. This bridge replaced a level crossing (*see 1900 Ordnance Survey map p. 110*).   *Author*

The rather ugly replacement signal box at Limerick station in July 1993. Note the rails are still bull-head in section with chairs. Long welded flat-bottomed rails are gradually being introduced in Ireland.   *Author*

The splendid station frontage and car park at Limerick in July 1993.   *Author*

a clerestory gable; and a smaller version of this covers the part of the site not now occupied with platforms. A siding extends between platforms 2 and 3 for a great part of the way, to enable short trains to be pushed out of the way to make room for the arrival of other trains at platform 2. To the north of the station a huge depot with many sidings and a huge travelling crane straddling them dominates the scene; the crane is higher than the station roof. A large signal box is sited beyond the far end of platforms 1 and 2. The station mostly receives and dispatches trains to Limerick Junction only, apart from the two each way (one in the winter months) serving the former W&LR line, but the making of a spur to the east of Limerick Junction now allows through running to and from Dublin without reversal, and some trains now do this; one of them, running only on certain days of the week,was extended to Ennis, the whole train reversing in the terminus and taking the leftward curve across the bridge over the Shannon.

The goods yard on the right-hand side of the Kerry line on a graded curve was the main GS&WR one, and sometimes called the Cork Direct Yard. In later days it was used for cement, grain and livestock traffic.

The Limerick Works, in later years reduced to just a wagon works, was half a mile from the station, adjacent to the ticket-checking platform on the up (arrival) side which remained in use until 15th June, 1963, the very last such platforms in the whole of the British Isles. The signal box at this point was called 'Limerick Check Cabin'.

From a point near the goods shed at Limerick a short line, the Market Siding, was opened on 23rd July, 1860, which crossed three streets on the level to serve the Market and two bacon factories. First worked by a small W&LR 0-4-0T, it was then operated with horses; later the GSR engines *Elf* and *Imp* were used, and just before closure in 1930 a Sentinel geared locomotive.

Chapter Nine

W&LR Locomotives
and Coaching Stock

According to the yearly statements put out by the Board of the W&LR and published in Bradshaw's *Shareholders' Guide*, 11 persons were named as locomotive superintendents during the 54 years of the company's independent existence. Between 1850 and 1859 no names were specified. Before that one name appears in 1848, indicating that he held that office during the previous year: William Martley; he, however, was only there for a few months and then resigned to take up a similar position on the South Devon Railway, finishing his career as locomotive superintendent at Longhedge Works, on the London Chatham & Dover Railway.

One may divide that period of 54 years into four parts: an early and undistinguished one during which no special locomotive policy or particular initiative was shown by those who held the superintendency, locomotives being bought 'off the peg' from builders in England as needed, or obtained second-hand. The second period, from 1862 to 1872 saw an efficient and strong-minded man in office, Martin Atock; who held sway at Limerick for 11 years while the equally strong-minded William Malcomson was Chairman of the line. According to a recent history of the GS&WR, which devotes a chapter to the W&LR, his period of superintendency

> . . . was one of financial difficulty, but [he] managed to rebuild the wagon stock and to keep his mixed fleet of locomotives on the road. By a skilful re-casting of the timetable in 1866 he cut engine mileage by some hundreds daily and saved the company £1,500 per annum. He continually importuned the Board for money, but was almost always refused; on occasions he had to remind the Directors that costs could be reduced no lower as his men would not work for less than one shilling and sixpence a day.*

Atock went on to hold the same position at Broadstone on the larger Midland Great Western Railway (MGWR), and from 1873 to 1882 the men who succeeded him at Limerick were comparative nonentities. The fourth and last period began with Henry Appleby who held office from 1883 to 1889 and ended with the reign of John G. Robinson, the most capable and prestigious of them all, who after leaving Ireland went on to add great distinction to his name by being (apart from a couple of years at the beginning of its existence) the Great Central Railway's (GCR) only chief mechanical engineer; there he earned fame by the quality and performance of the engines he built - the 4-4-0 'Directors' in particular, and when the GCR was merged in the London & North Eastern Railway in 1923 he was offered the chief position at Doncaster, but felt he was too old and preferred to resign.† Appleby came from the Monmouthshire Railway after it had been absorbed into the GWR; Robinson, having begun his engineering career at Swindon as an apprentice in 1872, went to Limerick to be Appleby's assistant in 1884, where his abilities marked him out to succeed his chief when the latter retired.

---

* K.A. Murray & D.B. McNeill: *The Great Southern and Western Railway*, 1976, p. 114.
† For a full account of Robinson's career, see *J.G. Robinson, A Lifetime's Work* by David Jackson, Oakwood Press, 1996.

WL&WR 2-4-0 No. 8 built in 1882 by the Vulcan Foundry, rebuilt by J.G. Robinson and named *Primrose*. Photographed at Limerick on 4th September, 1900.   *LCGB/Ken Nunn Collection*

WL&WR 2-4-0 No. 11 built in 1853 by Fairbairn & Sons and subsequently rebuilt by Robinson. Note that no cab has been added; also the raised firebox and wooden brake blocks. Photographed on 3rd September, 1900.   *LCGB/Ken Nunn Collection*

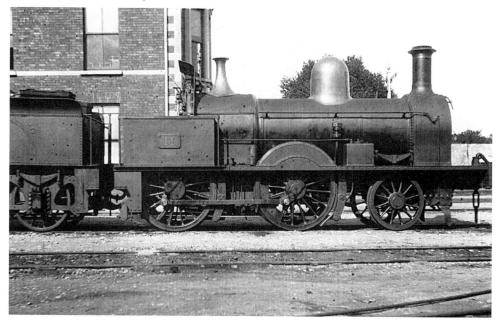

Details in regard to the W&LR's earlier locomotives such as dimensions and boiler pressure, are somewhat scanty. The first half-dozen, obtained when the line was opened, were outside-cylindered 2-2-2s built by Stothert and Slaughter of Bristol; in addition, four more engines were bought from William Dargan at the end of the period when he ran the line under contract. In regard to the locomotives from Bristol, most unusually a photograph exists, taken at Clonmel in 1858 and published in an illustrated book of Clonmel and its surroundings compiled by a Clonmel doctor, of one of these engines at the head of a westbound mixed train standing in Clonmel station. This is possibly the earliest railway photograph taken in Ireland to have survived.

These six engines all bore names, *Glengall, Bessborough, Waterford, Limerick, Suir, Shannon*, but were later simply numbered 1-6, the names being removed. They had 5 ft 9 in. diameter driving wheels, and were suitable for hauling light passenger trains but hardly powerful enough to tackle heavy freight; accordingly two 2-4-0s were also obtained from Fairbairn & Sons of Manchester and a number of mixed traffic engines of the same wheel arrangement from the Vulcan Foundry, Newton-le-Willows; these had 5 ft 6 in. diameter coupled wheels and 16 in. x 24 in. cylinders. Some of the latter were still at work in 1900 and passed into GS&WR ownership. Following this, several 0-4-2s were obtained at different times during 1853-1862, specifically for goods traffic; some were built by Sharp, Stewart & Co. of Manchester, others by Kitson & Co. of Leeds; all had 4 ft 6 in. diameter coupled wheels and 16 in. x 24 in. cylinders. A number of them were later rebuilt by Robinson at Limerick as four-coupled tank engines or 0-6-0 goods engines. In 1876 the Avonside Engine Company of Bristol built four larger locomotives with this wheel arrangement, with similarly-sized cylinders and 5 ft 3 in. diameter coupled wheels. These were sometimes used on passenger trains, and Robinson reconstructed one as a tank engine in 1899.

The first 0-6-0 did not appear until 1883 during Appleby's superintendency, when the Vulcan Foundry supplied two. With 5 ft 2 in. diameter coupled wheels and 17½ in. x 26 in. cylinders, these were at the time of their introduction the most powerful engines the W&LR possessed.

This constituted the company's locomotive stock in the year when Appleby took over. All were six-wheelers of one kind or another. In 1886 Appleby designed a 4-4-0 with 5 ft 6 in. diameter coupled wheels and 17½ in. x 26 in. cylinders, and one was built by the Vulcan Foundry. He followed it with another of the same wheel arrangement but with slightly smaller coupled wheels and cylinders; this was built by Dübs & Co. of Glasgow. His third design was another 0-6-0, also built by Dübs & Co., with 4 ft 6 in. diameter coupled wheels and 16 in. x 24 in. cylinders, which also came out in 1886. These were the only new engines built by Appleby.

So far there had been much variation and no standardisation in the W&LR's locomotive stock. After Robinson's succession to the locomotive superintendency standardisation began, along with other changes. One may mention first of all his introduction of a new livery for locomotives and coaches. The earliest W&LR engines had been painted green; this had then given place to brown, lined in blue and edged with yellow, with copper-topped chimneys and domes and nameplates of polished brass. This was certainly an unusual livery; imagination suggests it may not have been aesthetically very pleasing; at any rate, Robinson

WL&WR No. 44 *Nephin* designed by J.G. Robinson and built in 1893 by Dübs photographed at Waterford on 6th September, 1901. Note the re-railing jack beside the smokebox. Later numbered 291, this engine remained at work until 1959, the last W&LR locomotive in service.

LCGB/Ken Nunn Collection

Sister engine No. 23 *Slieve na Mon*, by now nameless and renumbered 276, is seen at Limerick on 30th April, 1938.

W.A. Camwell

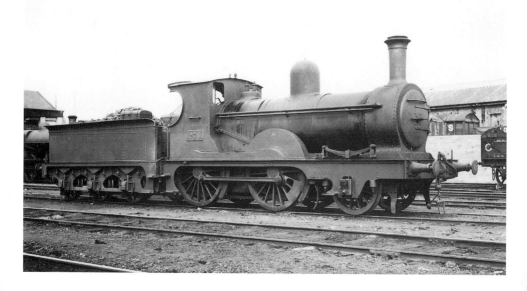

WL&WR saddle tank No. 1, purchased from Robert Stephenson & Co. in 1884 as a tender engine, is seen shunting coaches at Limerick on 31st August, 1901. *LCGB/Ken Nunn Collection*

0-4-4T locomotive No. 15 *Roxborough* as running in 1897. Built as an 0-4-2 tender engine by Sharp, Stewart in 1859, she had been rebuilt as a tank engine at Limerick Works in 1894, and incorporated the bogie off the Appleby 4-4-0 No. 12 (which was converted to a 2-4-0). No. 15 became GS&WR No. 268 and was scrapped in 1914. *R.W. Miller Collection*

WL&WR 2-4-0 No. 31 *Myrtle* photographed on 31st August, 1901; in poor condition but still with a brightly polished dome.   *LCGB/Ken Nunn Collection*

WL&WR 2-4-0 No. 37 *Camelia*, sister to *Lily* and *Myrtle* at Limerick on 31st August, 1901, rebuilt with a straight running plate.   *LCGB/Ken Nunn Collection*

0-4-2 No. 27 built by Avonside in 1876 at Limerick twenty years later. In 1899 this engine was rebuilt in Limerick Works as an 0-4-4T with the name *Thomond*.   *L&GRP*

The same engine, now GSR No. 279 and without the name, lasted in service until 1953 and is shown here after repairs and repainting at Inchicore on 25th April, 1938.   *W.A. Camwell*

Two views of 0-4-2T No. 3 *Zetland*. In the photograph above the engine is seen at Killaloe.
(Both) L&GRP

decided on a change, and from 1889 a new colour scheme was adopted. Passenger and (at first) goods locomotives were liveried in crimson lake, banded in black and with gold lining-out. The copper chimney caps and polished brasswork were retained (though only the passenger engines had polished domes) while the company's coat of arms adorned the tender centres (or, in the case of tank engines, the upper parts of the cab above tank-level) and cast number plates were set on the cab (or bunker) sides. Later on goods locomotives were painted black instead of red but similarly lined out. The consequence was the most attractive locomotive livery to be found in Ireland at that time, and it is a pity that it did not outlast the century, after which, the line having been absorbed into the GS&WR, the latter's livery was applied, black lined out with red and white lines, which was not exactly gorgeous; then, with the coming of World War I, battleship grey without lining replaced the black.

In commenting on the engines produced by Robinson for the W&LR, later the WL&WR, those designed but not actually built by him will first be mentioned; after that those constructed at Limerick Works will be dealt with. These latter were sometimes reconstructions of existing engines, and in some cases amounted to almost complete replacement, with almost none of the original engine being re-used.

Robinson's first design was a 2-4-0 for the main line services between Waterford and Limerick. It seems on the face of it curious that he should have reverted to this wheel arrangement when his predecessor had built 4-4-0s; possibly the fact that the latter were not all that successful in practice may have had something to do with it. In any case he managed to get a sizeable boiler and large firebox and firegrate fitted on to the six-wheel frame without placing undue weight on any of the wheels. For the first time in the company's history coupling splashers were fitted outside the wheel splashers. Eight of these engines were built by Dübs & Co. between 1889 and 1894. In them Robinson produced a very useful locomotive, which had (for contemporary Ireland) quite a turn of speed, despite the fact that the W&LR ran no non-stop journeys over 22 miles. E.L. Ahrons once timed one to achieve 64 mph on the down gradient between Tipperary and Cahir. In the new livery, with polished brasswork, hauling a train of crimson lake coaches, one of these would have presented a splendid sight. They coped well with the main line passenger services until the end of the century, and one of them managed to survive until 1959, outlasting the three companies to which it had successively belonged.

Robinson's next engines were a pair of 2-4-2 tanks - the first tank locomotives to be built for this company. They were intended for service on the branch from Limerick to Tralee, where they were more suited than tender engines because of the need to turn on the turntable at Newcastle West, whereas a tank could run as well backwards as forwards. These presaged other tank locomotives following a policy of using tender locomotives only on the main line between Limerick and Waterford. These locomotives were constructed by the Vulcan Foundry and many of their parts were interchangeable with the corresponding parts, including cylinders and boilers, of the older 'Flower' class of 2-4-0s which had also been supplied by the Vulcan Foundry between 1874 and 1882. This was the first sign of a policy of standardisation which was now being followed.

WL&WR 0-6-0 No. 2 *Shannon* built to J.G. Robinson's design in 1900, photographed at Limerick on 31st August, 1901. Note the Belpaire firebox.   *LCGB/Ken Nunn Collection*

Completed by Kitson & Co. in 1900 as WL&WR No. 4 *Shamrock*, as seen here, this was one of two Robinson 0-6-0s sold instead to the Midland Great Western Railway in 1901 for £3,200 each.
L&GRP

These 2-4-2s were unusual in having different types of bearings for their leading and trailing axles; at the front end the axleboxes were of the sliding type, but at the rear radial trucks were fitted, of the pattern developed by F.W. Webb on the London & North Western Railway. Both engines were sent to Tralee Shed and each made the double journey to Limerick and back each 24 hours, reversing at Newcastle West. After passing into G&SWR ownership one was eventually sold to the Cork and Macroom Direct Railway and ended its life there; the other, with altered smokebox doors which ruined its appearance, eventually went to Dublin in Great Southern Railways days, was withdrawn in 1935 and ended its days in Broadstone Shed, Dublin, where it was used to supply steam for washing-out purposes.

Next came a sequence of 0-6-0s, designed at Limerick and built by Dübs & Co. and Kitson & Co. in 1893-1895 and 1897 respectively. A further one followed these seven in 1900; with this for the first time the Belpaire firebox was introduced on a major Irish railway. (One had already been installed on a narrow-gauge line 12 years earlier.) These became the standard freight locomotives on the WL&WR and resembled the new 2-4-0s in the sizes of their boilers, fireboxes, firegrates and cylinders - a further instalment of standardisation; the tenders, however, were rather different, being made to hold more coal and less water. They became the mainstay of the company's freight services, supplementing a few rebuilds of earlier 0-6-0s. All passed to the GS&WR in 1901; some were withdrawn in 1911 and 1919; others survived to be included in GSR stock and lasted to between 1928 and 1951.

Robinson's last design of tender locomotive was a 4-4-0, of which three were built in 1896-1897 by Kitson & Co. They had swing-link bogies and were slightly heavier than their 2-4-0 precursors, though no more powerful, their chief dimensions being the same except that the heating surface in the boiler tubes was a tenth less than that of the earlier engines. They were used on the boat trains, which also carried perishables in vans, and seem to have coped well. A noticeable feature was the absence of smokebox wing plates that earlier locomotives had possessed. After they had passed to the GS&WR two were remodelled, being given boilers similar to those of the 2-4-0s and 0-6-0s, built-up chimneys that lacked the delicate curvature of Robinson's design, and square cab windows. All passed into GSR stock; one was withdrawn in 1928 and two lasted till 1949. The installation of a front bogie when there was no concomitant enlargement of the boiler is something of a puzzle. A possible clue is the practice, on the WL&WR, of carrying re-railing jacks on locomotives. A bogie engine might be expected not to de-rail as readily as one with a more rigid wheel base. As delays to the mail trains would have had more serious consequences than delays to other trains, this may account for the bogies - though even these engines carried their jacks around with them, as photographs show.

Robinson's next tank design to be put out to an English builder was an 0-4-4, of which Kitson & Co. built two in 1895; he had already, as recounted below, built a single one at Limerick. These were intended for the northward extension. They were given the full livery of crimson lake with polished brasswork and looked extremely handsome. The side tanks were rather low topped and smokebox wing-plates were provided. After they passed to the GS&WR the tops of the tanks were raised to the level of the cab windows, which

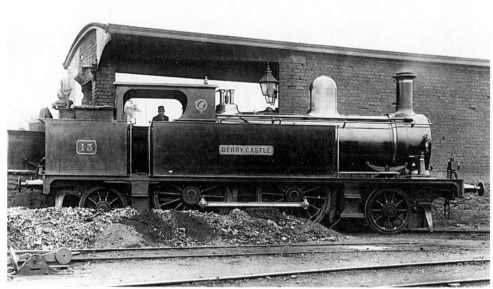

2-4-2T No. 13 *Derry Castle* was one of a pair designed by J.G. Robinson and introduced in 1891 for working trains between Limerick and Tralee, it is seen here in 1896.   *L&GRP*

No. 13 was sold to the Cork & Macroom Railway by the GS&WR in 1914 and it is seen here at Cork Capwell renumbered as No. 6.   *LCGB/Ken Nunn Collection*

2-4-2T No. 14 *Loch Derg*, a tank engine version of the 'Flower' class 2-4-0s, and seen at Tralee in the mid-1890s, was built in 1891 and lasted until 1935. *L&GRP*

WL&WR 4-4-2T No. 16 *Rocklands*, designed by J.G. Robinson and built by Kitson & Co. in 1896 and photographed at Limerick on 3rd September, 1900. It saw regular servie on the Limerick to Tralee line. *LCGB/Ken Nunn Collection*

Robinson express 4-4-0 No. 53 *Jubilee* was built by Kitson & Co. on 1896 and photographed at Limerick by H.L. Hopwood on 3rd September, 1900. Renumbered 296 by the GS&WR, this locomotive lasted until 1950.   *L&GRP*

Robinson 4-4-0 No. 55 *Bernard* soon after being renumbered by the GS&WR as No. 298 in 1901 and yet retaining her name for the time being. She was to remain in service until 1949. *L&GRP*

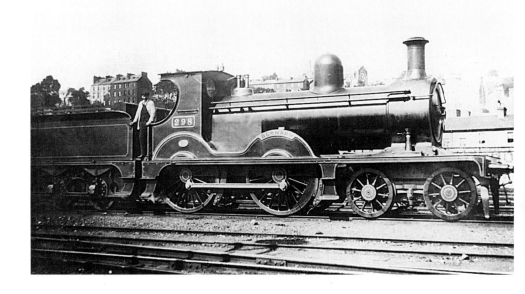

were made square, the wing plates were discarded, the characteristic Robinson chimneys with their delicate curvature were replaced by built-up ones, and a different design of smokebox door was fitted - all to the detriment of their appearance. One was scrapped as early as 1910; the other survived into GSR days, its last services being performed on the branch to Foynes. It was withdrawn in 1954, after a very long innings of nearly 60 years.

Robinson's last tank design entrusted to an outside builder included a front bogie. Four 4-4-2s were built by Kitson & Co. in 1896-1897. Similarly dimensioned to his 0-4-4s, they were intended for use on the Claremorris to Sligo extension, but were also used on the line from Limerick to Tralee. In full Robinson livery they looked very fine; GS&WR black took the shine off them and the later wartime grey made them even drabber. After this the GSR spoiled their appearance even further, raising the tank tops, replacing the coal rails with additional side sheeting and fixing new chimneys. In their later days they worked suburban trains from Dublin, and all ended their careers on the line between Cork and Bandon.

Robinson also built a few new locomotives at Limerick as well as reconstructing some earlier ones. In 1892 he built an 0-4-2 tank, his smallest engine, specifically for the service between Limerick and Killaloe. A photograph shows it to be quite a midget, with 4 ft 7 in. diameter coupled wheels, a low-pitched boiler, a tall chimney and a coal bunker so tiny that there was only just room for the number plate on either side. However, the short shuttle service it had to perform, only 17 miles each way, never took it far from coal supplies, and the side tanks would seem to have held enough water. It lasted for only 20 years, being withdrawn in 1912. Few dimensional details are known, but careful measurement of the photograph suggests that the rear carrying wheels were 3 ft 6 in. in diameter.

In 1894 an 0-4-4 tank engine was built at Limerick. It had short side tanks and smaller coupled wheels than Robinson's other 0-4-4s but a similarly-sized coal bunker. Like the other 0-4-4s it was used on the northern extension, and lasted until 1912. Its bogie had small wheels (measurement of the photograph suggests they were about 3 ft 1 in. in diameter) and the wheels had extended splashers - a feature Robinson did not perpetuate.

He also built three 0-6-0 goods engines as replacements for three earlier 0-4-2s, giving them smaller coupled wheels and cylinders an inch less in diameter. The GS&WR rebuilt them yet again before their withdrawal between 1905 and 1909.

All the locomotives on the line were named as well as numbered; in this respect they differed from those on the other larger Irish railways; the Great Northern Railway of Ireland and MGWR named some of their passenger engines, the Dublin Wicklow & Wexford and the GS&WR hardly any. The WL&WR evidently realised the publicity value of names, though some of those given to earlier engines seem somewhat peculiar. A number were of notables connected with the railway; others came from Irish legend or historic places in the area through which the line ran, or prominent geographical features. What was rather surprising was the fact that even freight engines were named. Even the publicity-conscious London, Brighton & South Coast Railway in Stroudley's day did not do this. A complete list of WL&WR locomotive names is given in Appendix One.

WL&WR 0-4-4-T No. 52 *Brian Boru* designed by J.G. Robinson, built in 1895 by Kitson & Co. and is photographed here at Sligo on 13th September, 1898. The starred headboard in front of the chimney indicates it has hauled a Sligo-bound train.   *LCGB/Ken Nunn Collection*

Nearly 30 years later No. 52, now renumbered 295, poses in the sunshine at Limerick on 30th April, 1938. Note the enlarged tanks and bunker, fitted in 1926. This locomotive was to continue working until 1954.   *W.A. Camwell*

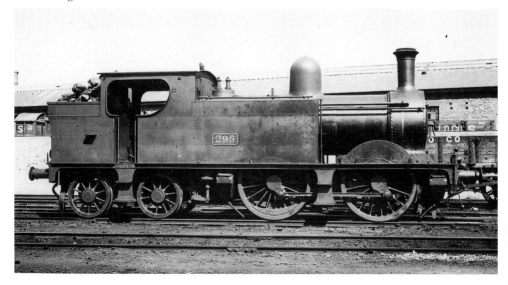

Brake third No. 36M was built in 1886 and is photographed at Foynes on 22nd April, 1955.
H.C. Casserley

The earliest coaches were four-wheelers (with the exception of some mentioned below) but later six-wheelers were built and by 1900 these composed the majority of passenger vehicles, though there were four bogie coaches, of recent construction, which were used on the trains connecting with the steamers to and from South Wales at Waterford. Two had short corridors and toilet compartments. A photograph exists of a former W&LR four-wheeled third class carriage; double footboards were common with Irish carriages in those days. In 1900 there were 159 coaches of which 60 were less than 10 years old. Many were electrically lit, which the GS&WR soon converted to gas.

A certain mystery surrounds some of the earliest coaches, which appear to have been mounted on a pair of bogies and to have been American in style. According to an article in the *Railway Magazine* of May 1964, R.B. Osborne, then the line's resident Engineer, introduced some for second and third class. In a report to the Directors written in 1847 he stated:

I have already submitted to the Board some of the facts which have led me to introduce on this line, with their sanction, this principle of carriage for the conveyance of passengers and goods; my experience has taught me that they are (especially for passengers) by far the safest means of conveyance that can be used on railways. They are also spacious, and therefore less confined; are better lighted; can be warmed in cold weather with an ordinary fireplace; and are more easy than any short carriage; and being strongly built afford protection and safety in case of accidents. The end platforms are made very strong and heavy, and so arranged that they receive the first concussion, and must be broken and crushed in before the end of the car itself can be injured.

Another view of coach No. 36M as it forms part of the 4.15 pm Foynes to Limerick train near Adare on 22nd April, 1955. 'J15' class No. 106 is at the head of the train.

H.C. Casserley

CIE No. 465A, formerly WL&WR 29 ft 10 in. family saloon (GSWR No. 900) was built in 1891 and withdrawn in 1963. It is seen here on 1st June, 1975 at Claremorris.

R.M. Casserley

These vehicles could not be coupled to normal ones (possibly having centre couplings) and it appears some goods vehicles on the same plan were built, GS&WR wagons were borrowed for through traffic. Osborne left the company in 1848 to return to the USA. A start was made to cut the carriages into four-wheelers each in 1849; two were moved to Boher and Bansha stations to act as temporary booking offices, but by 1851 all had gone. Meanwhile in 1851 the running of both locomotives and carriages had been handed over to the contractor William Dargan.

One may finally note that, for the conveyance of the lower orders, during the period when the line did not extend beyond Tipperary, open wagons were attached to some trains on certain days and designated as '4th class' accommodation. In them the impecunious could make the return journey from Tipperary for two shillings, sixpence less than if one took a third class ticket. Presumably some form of seating was provided.

The further history of locomotives and rolling stock over the W&LR lines belongs to the general history of the GS&WR. However, there was one item peculiar to the W&LR. In 1953 the Inchicore Works converted a 34-seat AEC bus to run on flanged wheels, a system already in use on the Great Northern Railway and Sligo, Leitrim & Northern Counties Railway. This was put to work in 1954 on the Thurles branch, but was taken off in 1956 because its seating capacity was insufficient on some days.

Timetable: W&LR Main Line: 1852

Mls.		Weekdays					Sundays
		a.m.	a.m.	p.m.	p.m.	p.m.	a m
	LIMERICK	6 00	10 45	1 00	4 30	7 00	11 45
4¼	Killonan	6 10		1 10	4 37		11 55
8	Boher	6 16	11 05	1 20	4 42	7 29	12 05
11¼	Dromkeen				4 51		12 16
13¾	Pallas	6 30	11 20	1 40	5 00	7 40	12 25
18¼	Oola	6 40		1 50	5 07		12 35
21¾	Limerick Junc.	7 00	11 45	2 10	5 25	8 20	12 50
	(dep.)	8 55	11 55	2 20	5 45	8 30	1 00
24¾	Tipperary	9 05	12 05	2 40	6 00	8 40	1 20
29½	Bansha	9 15	12 15	2 50	6 10	8 50	1 35
38¼	Cahir	9 40	12 35	3 10	6 35	9 10	1 55
49¼	CLONMEL	10 15	1 15	3 40	7 10	9 45	2 20

Mls.		Weekdays						Sundays
		a.m.	a.m.	a.m.	p.m.	p.m.	p.m.	a.m.
	CLONMEL	5 45		10 30	12 45	3 55	6 45	11 20
11	Cahir	6 10		10 55	1 10		7 10	11 55
19¾	Bansha	6 30		11 10	1 30	4 50	7 50	12 30
24½	Tipperary	6 45	8 35	11 20	1 45	5 00	8 00	12 40
27½	Limerick Junc.	7 00	8 45	11 40	2 05	5 20	8 25	12 50
	(dep.)		8 55	11 50	2 20	5 45	8 40	1 10
31	Oola		9 05	12 00		5 55		1 20
35½	Pallas		9 25	12 10	2 40	6 05	9 00	1 30
38	Dromkeen		9 35					1 40
41¼	Boher		9 45	12 25	2 50	6 30		1 50
45	Killonan		9 55	12 35	3 00	6 40	9 30	2 00
49¼	LIMERICK		10 05	12 45	3 10	7 00	9 40	2 10

Chapter Ten

Published Timetables for the Main Line
1852-1895

From various sources a sequence of published timetables for the line between Waterford and Limerick have been pieced together, at approximately 10-year intervals, which together show how the line's services developed during its years of independent operation. It seems best to present these and let them speak for themselves, with appropriate comments. The first timetable found is that printed in *Fisher's Irish Railway Time Table and General Advertiser* in 1852, which gave weekday and Sunday times together with the fares for all three classes between Limerick and all stations to Clonmel, to which point the railway had then been opened. Five trains ran in either direction, three being for first and second class passengers only; fares were 2*d*. a mile first class, 1½*d*. second class and 1*d*. third class, with day return tickets at half as much again as single fares. Rates are also given for the carriage of horses and carriages between certain of the stations, which was of course much more expensive as they required so much more room on the train; for example, one could go first class from Limerick to Clonmel for eight shillings, but to take a horse and a two-wheeled vehicle with you meant an extra expense of 36*s*., and if you travelled in style in a four-wheeler which needed three horses, 57*s*. was the charge. A dog, however, cost only a shilling, however far he went, though he was not permitted to travel with his owner.

Eleven years later the line had been extended to Waterford and the service had settled down to a pattern of four or five trains each way daily, with one or two going part-way only. The late night and early morning mail trains ran both on weekdays and Sundays, together with one daytime Sunday train in each direction. The average overall time between Waterford and Limerick was about 4 hours 10 minutes, sometimes with lengthy waits at Limerick Junction. The night trains, which took the mails, also had goods vehicles which might need to be attached or detached *en route*; hence their longer schedules. The most important service in each direction was the mid-morning one which ran in connection with the boat to or from South Wales. Eastbound and westbound trains mostly crossed at Limerick Junction, though the two mid-afternoon trains did so at Cahir.

The table for 1873 shows a reduction of through services to four each way - the consequence, no doubt, of Mr Atock's re-orderings. The two boat trains leave Waterford and Limerick a little later and are a little faster. Average overall time is about the same. It is noticeable that there are no longer any daytime Sunday trains; the sabbatarian Mr Malcomson has seen to their excision.

Nine years later the service had become more frequent, with the mid-morning westbound train from Waterford taking just over 3½ hours and a newly-introduced train in the early afternoon in the same direction being half an hour faster still. Eastbound, the mid-morning service from Limerick took just over 3¼ hours. Both the two latter trains ran non-stop from Limerick

TIMETABLE: W&LR MAIN LINE: 1863

Mls.		Weekdays						Sundays	
		a.m.	a.m.	a.m.	p.m.	p.m.	p.m	p.m.	p.m.
	LIMERICK		730	1100	400	600	1045	1210	1045
4¼	Killonan								
8	Boher		750	1115	420	625		1227	
11¼	Dromkeen		759		430			1237	
13¾	Pallas		808	1135	440	645	1130	1247	1130
18¼	Oola		820		455			100	
21¾	Limerick Junc.		835	1200	505	720	1200	110	1200
	(dep.)		845	1222	525		1215	130	1215
24¾	Tipperary		905	1235	545		1245	140	1245
29½	Bansha		915	1245	600			150	
38¼	Cahir		945	105	625		130	215	130
49¼	Clonmel		1020	132	650		215	240	215
55	Kilsheelan		1035		705			300	
63	Carrick-on-Suir	830	1100	203	730		255	325	255
67¼	Fiddown	845	1110	213	740		307	335	307
70	Grange	853	1120		748			345	
77¼	WATERFORD	910	1140	235	810		345	400	345

Mls		Weekdays						Sundays	
		a.m	a.m.	p.m.	p.m.	p.m.	p.m	a.m.	p.m.
	WATERFORD	600	945	235	415		830	1020	830
7¼	Grange	617			435			1040	
10	Fiddown	625	1005	255	445		909	1050	909
14¼	Carrick-on-Suir	640	1020	308	455		920	1100	920
22¼	Kilsheelan	657		325	520			1125	
28	Clonmel	715	1050	345	545		1000	1140	1000
39	Cahir	745	1120	415	625		1045	1215	1045
47¾	Bansha	805	1140	435				1235	
52½	Tipperary	815	1150	450	710		1130	1255	1130
55½	Limerick Junc.	835	1205	505	730		1200	110	1200
	(dep.)	845	1224	525		840	1215	130	1215
59	Oola	855		536				140	
63½	Pallas	905	1244	550		900	1240	150	1240
66	Dromkeen	915		557				200	
69¼	Boher	925	1258	605		920		210	
73	Killonan								
77¼	LIMERICK	945	120	630		950	120	230	120

TIMETABLE: W&LR MAIN LINE: 1873

Mls.		Weekdays						Suns.
		a.m.	a.m.	a.m.	p.m.	p.m.	p.m.	p.m.
	LIMERICK	600	700	1120	120	400	1040	1040
4¼	Killonan							
8	Boher	623		1138		420		
11¼	Dromkeen	633				430		
13¾	Pallas	643	740	1200		440	1110	1110
18¼	Oola	653				455		
21¾	Limerick Junc.	705	810	1220	220	515	1155	1155
	(dep.)	720	920	1230		535	1223	1223
24¾	Tipperary	735	940	1240		545	1250	1250
29½	Bansha	755		1250		600	105	105
38¼	Cahir	815		120		625	135	135
49¼	Clonmel	845		140		655	220	220
55	Kilsheelan	905				710		
63	Carrick-on-Suir	925		205		735	300	300
67¼	Fiddown	935		215		745	310	310
70	Grange	942				750		
77¼	WATERFORD	1010		245		815	345	345

Mls.		Weekdays						Suns.
		a.m.	a.m.	a.m.	a.m.	p.m.	p.m.	p.m.
	WATERFORD	545	850		1145	245	855	855
7¼	Grange	605				303		
10	Fiddown	615			1207	313	925	925
14¼	Carrick-on-Suir	625	935		1217	325	940	940
22¼	Kilsheelan	645				345		
28	Clonmel	705	1035		1245	404	1022	1022
39	Cahir	735			120	433	1057	1057
47¾	Bansha	755			137	455	1123	1123
52½	Tipperary	810		1040	150	509	1140	1140
55½	Limerick Junc.	820		1105	210	520	1155	1155
	(dep.)	830		1212	225	545	1223	1223
59	Oola	845				555		
63½	Pallas	855		1227	245	603	100	100
66	Dromkeen	905		1237		612		
69¼	Boher	920		1247	258	622		
73	Killonan							
77¼	LIMERICK	950		115	315	645	130	130

TIMETABLE: W&LR MAIN LINE: 1882

Mls. — Weekdays — Suns.

Mls.		a.m.	a.m.	a.m	p.m.	p.m.	p.m.	p.m.
	LIMERICK		7 00	11 00	1 35	4 00	10 50	10 50
4¼	Killonan							
8	Boher		7 18	11 18		4 20		
11¼	Dromkeen		7 28	11 28		4 30		
13¾	Pallas		7 35	11 35		4 40	11 15	11 15
18¼	Oola		7 50	11 50		4 55		
21¾	Limerick Junc.		8 10	12 05	2 15	5 15	11 55	11 55
	(dep.)		8 35	12 15	2 25	5 35	12 23	12 23
24¾	Tipperary		8 55	12 30	2 35	5 50	12 50	12 50
29½	Bansha		9 10	12 40	2 45	6 05	1 05	1 05
38¼	Cahir		9 35	1 05	3 05	6 30	1 35	1 35
49¼	Clonmel	7 30	10 05	1 32	3 30	7 00	2 20	2 20
55	Kilsheelan	7 55	10 22	1 45	3 45	7 20	2 35	2 35
63	Carrick-on-Suir	8 30	10 40	2 00	4 05	7 45	3 00	3 00
67¼	Fiddown	8 50	10 55	2 10	4 15	7 55	3 10	3 10
70	Grange	9 00				8 00		
77¼	WATERFORD	9 30	11 30	2 35	4 40	8 30	3 45	3 45

Mls. — Weekdays — Suns.

Mls.		a.m.	a.m.	a.m.	p.m.	p.m.	p.m.
	WATERFORD	6 00	9 35	11 35	2 45	8 30	8 30
7¼	Grange	Flag	9 50	Flag	3 03	Flag	Flag
10	Fiddown	6 20	9 57	11 57	3 13	9 00	9 00
14¼	Carrick-on-Suir	6 30	10 07	12 07	3 25	9 15	9 15
22¼	Kilsheelan	6 48	10 22	12 22	3 45	9 30	9 30
28	Clonmel	7 04	10 35	12 35	4 04	10 00	10 00
39	Cahir	7 30	11 00	1 05	4 33	11 15	11 15
47¾	Bansha	7 50	11 20	1 30	4 55	11 15	11 15
52½	Tipperary	8 05	11 35	1 45	5 09	11 35	11 35
55½	Limerick Junc.	8 25	11 50	2 00	5 20	11 50	11 50
	(dep.)	8 35	12 12	2 23	5 45	12 23	12 23
59	Oola	8 45		2 35	5 56		
63½	Pallas	8 55		2 45	6 05	12 50	12 50
66	Dromkeen	9 00		2 50	6 15		
69¼	Boher	9 10		3 00	6 30		
73	Killonan						
77¼	LIMERICK	9 35	12 52	3 25	6 50	1 30	1 30

Junction to Limerick, and vice versa, and their actual running times were very similar, since the westbound train had longer to wait at the Junction, where all passenger trains now crossed with one another. The average journey time between the two cities was now only just over four hours. Acceleration had been slow; it has to be remembered that there were goods trains to be waited for at some of the crossing places, and that one or two of the advertised trains were 'mixed' - the 7.30 am from Clonmel to Waterford, for example, which needed a full two hours for the 28 miles, because of long stops to attach or remove wagons and vans. Furthermore, the reorganisation of the locomotive stock by J.G. Robinson had not yet begun, and the engines available were still small, underpowered and insufficient in number, three also being single-wheelers.

One curiosity in this timetable is the number of 'flag' stops for westbound trains at Grange, there being none in the opposite direction; presumably the station attendant brought the train to a halt with a red flag if required, if it was not due to stop there. Yet Grange station was not near any place of any size, nor did any of the Directors live in the vicinity. What, one wonders, was the reason for this special treatment at this time?

Finally, the services for 1895. One is fortunate to have had access to the working timetable for November of this year, which shows much more than the public timetable and gives interesting additional information, such as the need to pass all facing points at no higher speed than 10 mph, and to go no faster than that over Dunkitt viaduct. Goods train movements as well as those of passenger trains are shown. Those which ran during the night hours required between 6 and 6½ hours to cover the whole distance, while the daytime goods train, eastbound, required as much as 10 hours, with long waits at Limerick Junction and Clonmel and an even longer one at Tipperary. 'Flag' stops have been discontinued at Grange but one has appeared at Boher, while the morning eastbound mail stops at Killonan and Pallas when required to pick up passengers, the warning being given not by flags but by signals. Killonan offers something of a puzzle. Only one train, the first eastbound one of the day, is clearly booked to stop there; the small printed numbers with the other trains suggest passing times. Can it possibly have been so little used?

The average time for passenger trains between the two terminals has now come down to an average of under 3½ hours, with one eastbound service doing it in less than three. One westbound train also manages the 21¼ miles from Limerick Junction to a ticket-check stop outside Limerick in 33 minutes; allowing for the need to back and reverse at the Junction, this is the system's first 40 mph booking. The route was of course entirely downhill, and double-tracked in those days. One may attribute the general speed-up to the use of Mr Robinson's new locomotives.

The 1895 timetable no doubt represents the general picture of train services during the final decade of the company. They were not to improve as time went on, after the line had been taken over by the GS&WR, which was backing another horse so far as the boat trains were concerned. The 'nineties' were the line's short lived period of briskness - 'brilliance' would hardly be the word. The next chapter traces the period of decline and describes the situation at the present day.

UP TRAINS—Waterford to Thurles Branch and Limerick.

Distance from Waterford.	STATIONS.		WEEK-DAYS. 1 Goods.	2 Mixed.	3 Passenger. Mail.	4 Goods.	5 Passenger.	6 Passenger, Mail.	Week-Days. 7 Mixed to Tipperary.	8 Mixed. Mail.	9 Goods except Saturdays.	SUNDAYS. 1 Passenger.	2 Mixed.	3 Goods.	STATIONS.	Distance from Waterford.
			A.M.	A.M.	A.M.	P.M.	A.M.	P.M.	P.M.	P.M.	P.M.	P.M.	P.M.	P.M.		
	WATERFORD	dep	3 0	...	7 10	...	10 20	1 50	3 10	9 0	11 30	...	9 0	11 30	WATERFORD	
7¼	GRANGE	arr	3 22	...	7 25	...	...	2 1	3 25	9 17		...	9 17	...	GRANGE	7¼
		dep	3 27	...	7 26	...	...	2 2	3 26	9 18		...	9 18	...		
** 10	FIDDOWN	arr	3 40	...	7 33	...	10 38	2 8	3 32	9 25	12 10	...	9 25	12 10	FIDDOWN	10
		dep	4 0	...	7 34	...	10 39	2 9	3 33	9 26	12 12	...	9 26	12 12		
** 14¼	CARRICK	arr	4 12	...	7 43	...	10 46	2 16	3 42	9 35	12 29	...	9 35	12 29	CARRICK	14¼
		dep	4 32	...	7 46	...	10 48	2 18	3 44	9 38	12 40	...	9 38	12 40		
	KILSHEELAN	arr	4 54	..	8 2	...	11 3	2 34	4 0	9 55	1 10	...	9 55	1 10	KILSHEELAN	22
** 22		dep	5 0	...	8 3	...	11 5	2 36	4 3	9 58	1 20	...	9 58	1 20		
	CLONMEL (Thurles Jct.)		5 19	..	8 15	...	11 15	2 48	4 14	10 14	1 43	..	10 14	1 43	CLONMEL (Thurles Jct.) Pass	
** 28	CLONMEL...	arr	5 20	...	8 16	...	11 16	2 50	4 15	10 15	1 45	...	10 15	1 45	CLONMEL	2
	SOUTHERN LINE.		Goods.	Mixed.			Passr.		Passr.						*SOUTHERN LINE.*	
* 28	CLONMEL	dep	11 0	7 0	..	...	11 25	..	4 25	...	...	...	...	...	CLONMEL	28
			A													
* 36½	FETHARD	arr.	11 20	7 20	..	...	11 44	...	4 42	...	...	...	...	...	FETHARD	36½
		dep	11 53	7 25	...	...	11 46	...	4 45	...	...	...	..	...		
39½	FARRANALLEEN ...	arr	12 0	7 32	...	...	11 53	...	4 51	...	...	...	...	...	FARRANALLEEN	39½
		dep	12 4	7 34	..	...	11 54	...	4 53	...	...	...	...	..		
* 44	LAFFAN'S BRIDGE	arr	12 14	7 45	...	...	12 4	...	5 3	...	...	.	...	...	LAFFANSBRIDGE	44
		dep	12 23	7 47	...	...	12 6	...	5 5	...	...	...	...	...		
47¾	HORSE AND JOCKEY	arr	12 33	7 57	...	...	12 17	...	5 13	...	...	...	...	..	HORSE & JOCKEY	47¾
		dep	12 38	8 3	...	...	12 20	..	5 16	...	...	...	..	...		
* 53½	THURLES	arr	12 53	8 20	...	...	12 35	...	5 33	...	...	...	...	...	THURLES...	53½
			Goods.						Mixed.							
** 28	CLONMEL	dep	5 37	...	8 20	...	11 18	3 0	4 20	10 20	2 15	...	10 20	2 15	CLONMEL	28
	CLONMEL (North Box)		5 38	...	8 21	..	11 19	3 1	4 21	10 21	2 16	...	10 21	2 16	CLONMEL (North Box) ...	
** 39	CAHER	arr	6 11	...	8 45	...	11 36	3 18	4 42	10 48	2 55	...	10 48	3 0	CAHER	39
		dep	6 31	...	8 50	...	11 39	3 19	4 45	10 52	3 20	...	10 52	3 25		
** 47¾	BANSHA	arr	6 51	...	9 10	..	11 53	3 33	5 3	11 12	3 45	...	11 12	3 50	BANSHA	47¾
		dep	7 1	.	9 11	...	11 54	3 34	5 4	11 13	3 50	...	11 13	4 0		
** 52½	TIPPERARY	arr	7 15	...	9 21	...	12 3	3 43	5 14	11 30	4 10	...	11 30	4 20	TIPPERARY	52½
		dep	Mixed 7 47	...	9 26	1 20	12 5	3 45	5 20	11 35	4 25	...	11 35	4 35		
55¼	LIMK.JUNC.Keanes Pnts ...		8 0	...	9 38	1 30	12 13	3 54	5 28	11 48	4 38	...	11 48	4 48	LK. JUNC. (Keane's Points)	55¼
** 55½	LIMERICK JUNCTION	arr	8 2	...	9 40	1 32	12 15	3 55	5 30	11 50	4 40	...	11 50	4 50	LIMERICK JUNCTION	55½
		dep	8 25	..	9 58	1 50	12 30		5 52	12 23	5 5	1 50	12 23	5 15		
59	OOLA	arr	8 35	...	...	2 0	12 38	...	6 0	...	..	1 58	...	...	OOLA	59
		dep	8 37	...	...	2 10	12 40	...	6 1	...	...	1 59	...	...		
63½	PALLAS	arr	8 47	..	...	2 20	12 49	4 9	6 9	12 43	...	2 7	12 43	...	PALLAS	63½
		dep	8 50	...	...	2 32	12 51	4 11	6 10	12 45	...	2 8	12 45	...		
66	DROMKEEN	arr	8 55	...	...	...	12 56	...	6 15	...	...	2 13	...	..	DROMKEEN	66
		dep	8 57	...	...	...	12 57	...	6 16	...	...	2 14	...	...		
69¼	BOHER	arr	9 7	...	..	Flag.	1 4	...	6 22	...	...	2 20	..	...	BOHER	69¼
		dep	9 10	...	...	...	1 5	...	6 23	...	...	2 22	...	...		
73	KILLONAN		9 20	...	10 24	3 0	1 13	4 39	6 29	1 7	5 48	2 28	1 7	6 3	KILLONAN	73
			...	...	...	...	...		...	...	...	...	...	...		
76½	ENNIS JUNCTION		9 29		10 30	3 8	1 19	4 45	6 35	1 14	5 58	2 34	1 14	6 13	ENNIS JUNCTION...	76½
76¾	LIMERICK CHECK ...	arr	9 30	...	10 31	...	1 20	4 46	6 36	1 15	...	2 35	1 15	...	LIMERICK CHECK	76¾
		dep	9 33	..	10 33	...	1 23	4 48	6 38	1 18	...	2 38	1 18	..		
77¼	LIMERICK	arr	9 35	...	10 35	3 10	1 25	4 50	6 40	1 20	6 0	2 40	1 20	6 15	LIMERICK	77¼

Stations marked thus (**) are Electric Staff Stations.
Stations marked thus (*) are Train Staff and Ticket Stations.
Bars across the Lines thus (=) denote the places where trains cross or pass each other
A Runs only on Mondays, Wednesdays and Fridays, between Clonmel and Thurles

Speed of all Trains when passing over Viaducts at Dunkitt (near Waterford), and also all Facing Points, not to exceed 10 miles an hour.
The Times shown for Ennis Junction, Killonan, "Keane's Points," Limerick Junction Clonmel North Box, and Clonmel Thurles Junction are the times trains are due to pass.

Week Days.—No. 1—To pass No. 9 Down at Carrick, No. 1 Down at Limerick Junction.
No. 3—To pass No. 1 Down at Caher, and pass No. 4 Down at Tipperary, and No. 2 Down at Limerick Junction.
No. 5—To pass No. 2 Down at Kilsheelan, and No. 3 Down at Limerick Junction, and No. 4 Down at Bansha.
No. 6—To pass No. 4 Down at Clonmel and No. 5 Down at Limerick Junction.

Week Days.—No. 7—To pass No. 4 Down at Kilsheelan, No. 5 Down at Caher, and No. 6 Down at Limerick Junction.
No. 8—To pass Nos. 8 and 9 Down at Limerick Junction.
No. 9—To pass No. 8 Down at Clonmel and No. 9 Down at Caher.
Sundays.—No. 2—To pass No 2 Down at Limerick Junction.
No. 3—To pass No. 2 Down at Clonmel.

Extract from the WL&WR Working Timetable of November 1895.

Week Days.—No. 1—To pass No. 1 up at Limerick Junction.
No. 2—To pass No. 3 Up at Limerick Junction, precede No. 4 Down from Tipperary, and pass No. 5 Up at Kilsheelan
No. 3—To pass No. 5 Up at Limerick Junction.
No. 4—To pass No. 3 Up at and follow No. 2 Down from Tipperary, pass No. 5 Up at Bansha, No. 6 Up at Clonmel, and No. 7 Up at Kilsheelan.
No. 5—To pass No. 6 Up at Limerick Junction and No. 7 Up at Caher.

DOWN TRAINS—Limerick and Thurles to Waterford.

Distance from Limerick.	STATIONS.		WEEK-DAYS.	1 Passenger.	2 Passenger Mail.	3 Mixed.	4 Goods.	5 Passenger Mail.
			A.M.	A.M.	A.M.	A.M.	A.M.	P.M.
	LIMERICK	dep	...	7 0	9 10	11 5	7 20	3 10
	ENNIS JUNCTION	pass	...	7 2	9 12	11 7	7 22	3 12
4¼	KILLONAN	arr	...	7 8	9 18	...	...	...
		dep	...	7 9	B	11 16	7 31	3 18
8	BOHER	arr	...	7 17	...	11 24	7 40	...
		dep	...	7 18	...	11 25	7 42	...
11¼	DROMKEEN	arr	...	7 25	...	11 32	7 50	...
		dep	...	7 26	..	11 33	...	...
13¾	PALLAS	arr	...	7 31	B	11 38	7 55	...
		dep	...	7 32		11 40	8 5	...
18¼	OOLA	arr	...	7 40	...	11 50	8 15	...
		dep	...	7 42	...	11 55	8 25	...
·	L'CK J'CTN (Keane's Points)		...	7 50	9 49	12 3	8 33	3 48
** 21¾	LIMERICK JUNCTION	arr	...	7 52	9 50	12 5	8 35	3 50
		dep	...	8 3	10 0	12 30	9 5	4 7
** 24¾	TIPPERARY	arr	...	8 13	10 10	12 40	9 20	4 15
		dep	...	8 18	10 11		11 30	4 16
** 29½	BANSHA	arr	...	8 25	10 18	...	11 45	4 24
		dep	...	8 27	10 19	...	11 55	4 25
** 38¼	CAHER	arr	...	8 43	10 32	...	12 15	4 40
		dep	...	8 48	10 35	...	2 0	4 44
	CLONMEL (North Box)		...	9 11	10 51	..	2 28	5 6
** 49¼	CLONMEL	arr	...	9 12	10 52	...	2 30	5 7
	SOUTHERN LINE.				Passr.		Goods.	Mixed.
* 74¾	THURLES	dep	...	...	9 20	...	1 0	2 30
69	HORSE & JOCKEY ...	arr	...	...	9 32	...	A 1 13	2 43
		dep	...	...	9 34	...	1 20	2 44
* 65¼	LAFFANSBRIDGE ...	arr	...	...	9 43	...	1 33	2 53
		dep	...	...	9 44	...	1 40	2 54
60¾	FARRANALLEEN ...	arr	...	...	9 55	...	1 52	3 6
		dep	...	...	9 57	...	1 55	3 7
* 57¾	FETHARD...	arr	...	...	10 3	...	2 2	3 17
		dep	...	...	10 11	...	2 15	3 20
* 49¼	CLONMEL	arr	...	...	10 30	...	2 30	3 40
					Passr.		Goods.	
** 49¼	CLONMEL	dep	..	9 16	10 54	...	3 30	5 10
	CLONMEL PASS (Thurles Jct)		...	9 17	10 55	..	3 31	5 11
** 55	KILSHEELAN	arr	...	9 27	11 4	...	3 55	5 20
		dep	..	9 28	11 7	...	4 5	5 21
** 63	CARRICK	arr	...	9 45	11 26	...	4 30	5 32
		dep	...	9 47	11 28	...	4 40	5 33
** 67¼	FIDDOWN	arr	...	9 56	11 35	...	4 50	5 41
		dep	...	9 57	11 36	...	4 55	5 42
70	GRANGE	arr	...	10 3	...	...	...	...
		dep	...	10 4	...	...	...	
76½	WATERFORD CHECK	arr	...	10 20	12 0	...	...	6 5
		dep	...	10 23	12 2	...	...	6 7
77¼	WATERFORD ...	arr	...	10 25	12 5	...	5 20	6 10

Stations marked thus (**) are Electric Staff Stations.
Bars across the Lines thus (=) denote the places where trains cross or pass each other.
Stations marked thus (*) are Train Staff and Ticket Stations.
A Runs between Thurles and Clonmel only on Mondays, Wednesdays and Fridays.
B Stops at Killonan and Pallas when required.
When no Passengers offer, Signals to be lowered for train to run through.

Week-Days. 6 Passenger.	7 Goods Saturdays only.	8 Mixed. Mail.	9 Goods except Saturdays.	10 Goods Saturdays only.	SUNDAYS. 1 Passenger.	2 Mixed. Mail.	STATIONS.	Distance from Limerick.
P.M.	P.M.	P.M.	P.M.	P.M.	NOON.	P.M.		
4 25	9 0	11 0	11 20	11 40	12 0	11 0	LIMERICK	
4 27	9 3	11 3	11 23	11 43	12 2	11 3	ENNIS JUNCTION ...	
...	...	...	...	...	...	...	KILLONAN	4¼
4 33	9 13	11 14	11 35	11 54	12 8	11 14		
4 41	...	...	...	...	12 16	...	BOHER	8
4 43	...	...	...	...	12 18	...		
4 49	...	...	...	...	12 25	...	DROMKEEN	11¼
4 51	...	11 30	11 59	...	12 26	..		
4 56	...	11 35	12 4	...	12 31	11 35	PALLAS	13¾
4 59	...	11 40	...	...	12 33	11 40		
5 9	...		...	...	12 41	...	OOLA	18¼
5 14	...		...	...	12 43	...		
5 23	9 56	11 58	12 35	12 58	12 48	11 58	L'K J'CT (K'ne's P'ts)	
5 25		12 0	12 37	1 0	12 50	12 0	LIMERICK JUNCTION	21¾
5 50	Pass	12 25	1 5	1 20	...	12 25		
6 0	10 2	12 40	1 20	1 35	...	12 40	TIPPERARY	24¾
6 5	10 10	12 50	1 40	1 45	...	12 50		
6 17	10 20	1 2	1 55	2 0	...	1 2	BANSHA	29½
6 20	10 21	1 3	2 5	2 1	...	1 3		
6 40	10 40	1 23	2 25	2 25	...	1 23	CAHER	38¼
6 45	10 50	1 28	3 0	2 30	..	1 28		
7 9	11 18	1 52	3 33	2 58		1 52	CLONMEL (N'rth B'x)	
7 10	11 20	1 53	3 35	3 0	...	1 53	CLONMEL	49¼
Passr.							SOUTHERN LINE.	
5 45	...	...	...	...	...	...	THURLES ...	74¾
5 57	..	...	...	...	...	...	HORSE & JOCKEY	69
5 59	...	...	...	...	...	...		
6 7	...	...	...	...	...	...	LAFFANSBRIDGE	65¼
6 10	...	...	...	...	...	...		
6 19	...	...	...	...	...	...	FARRANALLEEN	60¾
6 20	...	...	...	...	...	...		
6 27	...	...	...	...	...	...	FETHARD	57¾
6 30	...	...	...	...	...	...		
6 50	...	...	...	...	...	...	CLONMEL ...	49¼
Passr.								
7 15	11 30	2 3	3 50	3 10	...	2 3	CLONMEL	49¼
7 16	11 32	2 4	...	3 11		2 4	CLONMEL (Th'ls Jct)	
7 27	11 50	2 17	4 10	3 30	...	2 17	KILSHEELAN	55¼
7 28	11 51	2 18	4 12	3 31	...	2 18		
7 45	12 8	2 33	4 32	3 51	...	2 33	CARRICK	63
7 48	12 9	2 38	4 50	3 55	...	2 38		
7 55	12 18	2 47	5 0	4 5	...	2 47	FIDDOWN	67¼
7 56	12 19	2 48	5 5	...	...	2 48		
8 1	...	...	...	...	...	...	GRANGE	70
8 2	...	...	...	...	...	...		
8 19		3 10	...	...	...	3 1	WATERFORD CHECK	76½
8 22	...	3 12	...	...	...	3 12		
8 25	12 45	3 15	5 35	4 30	...	3 15	WATERFORD ..	77¼

The times shown for Ennis Junction, Killonan, "Keane's Points," Limerick Junction, Clonmel North Box and Clonmel Thurles Junction are the times trains are due to pass.

Week Days.—No. 6—To pass No. 7 Up at Limerick Junction.
No. 7—To pass No. 8 Up at Caher.
No. 8—To pass No. 8 at Up Limerick Junction and No. 9 Up at Clonmel.
No. 9—To pass No. 8 Up at Limerick Junction, follow No. 8 Down from Tipperary, and pass No. 9 Up at Caher and No. 1 Up at Carrick.
Sundays.—No 2—To pass No. 2 Up at Limerick Junction and No. 3 Up at Clonmel.

Extract from the WL&WR Working Timetable of November 1895.

UP TRAINS—Limerick to Foynes, Tralee and Fenit.

Distance from Limerick.	STATIONS.		WEEK-DAYS. 1 Mixed Mail.	2 G.S. & W. Pass.	3 Goods A	4 G.S. & W. Pass.	5 Pass. Mail.	6 Pass.	7 G.S. & W. Pass.	8 G.S. & W. Goods	9 G.S. & W. Goods	Sundays 1 Mixed Mail.
			A.M.	A.M.	A.M.	A.M.	A.M.	P.M.	P.M.	P.M.	P.M.	A.M.
*	LIMERICK ...	dep	4 50	6 40	7 0	10 30	10 50	5 40	5 20	7 0	9 30	7 30
¾	LIMERICK CHECK	arr	4 53	...	7 3	...	10 53	5 43	...	.	..	7 33
		dep	4 55	...	7 5	..	10 56	5 45	...	...	...	7 35
	FOYNES JUNCTION	PASS	4 56	6 41	7 7	10 31	10 57	5 46	5 21	7 1	9 31	7 36
* 7	PATRICKSWELL ..	arr	5 10	6 54	7 35	10 44	11 10	6 0	5 34	7 21	9 51	7 48
		dep	5 11	6 55	7 50	10 45	11 11	6 1	5 35	7 31	10 0	7 50
11	ADARE	arr	5 20	...	8 0	...	11 18	6 8	...	...	...	7 58
		dep	5 21	...	8 10	...	11 19	6 9	...	...	...	8 0
*17¼	BALLINGRANE	arr	5 38	...	**8 35**	..	11 31	6 24	...	...	...	8 15
	Foynes Line.				P.M.		Mixed					
*17¼	BALLINGRANE	dep	...	...	2 5	..	11 35	6 27	...	...	..	...
20¾	ASKEATON ...	arr	...	...	2 13	...	11 43	6 35	...	...	...	...
		dep	...	...	2 15	...	11 45	6 37	...	...	...	...
*26¾	FOYNES ...	arr	...	...	2 30	...	12 0	6 55	...	...	...	...
*17¼	BALLINGRANE	dep	5 40	...	**8 45**	...	11 33	**6 25**	...	...	...	8 18
*19¼	RATHKEALE ...	arr	5 45	...	8 55	...	11 37	6 30	...	...	...	8 23
		dep	5 50	...	9 15	...	11 38	6 31	...	...	..	8 28
24½	ARDAGH	arr	6 5	...	9 33	...	11 50	6 44	...	...	...	8 41
		dep	6 8	..	9 38	...	11 54	6 45	...	...	...	8 43
*27¼	NEWCASTLEWEST	arr	6 15	...	9 45	...	12 3	**6 52**	...	...	...	8 50
		dep	6 30	...	10 30	...	12 13	**7 2**	...	...	...	9 5
*33½	BARNAGH	arr	6 49	...	10 55	..	12 28	7 17	...	...	...	9 22
		dep	6 50	...	10 57	...	12 31	7 18	...	...	...	9 25
38	DEVONROAD ...	arr	7 2	...	11 10	No.	12 40	7 27	...	...	...	9 34
		dep	7 5	...	11 13	10	12 41	7 28	...	..	..	9 35
*41¼	ABBEYFEALE ...	arr	7 15	...	11 23	...	**12 50**	7 37	...	..	..	9 43
		dep	7 20	...	11 33	Fri-days	**12 53**	7 38	...	..	...	9 45
45¼	KILMORNA ...	arr	7 29	...	11 47	only	1 3	7 48	..	...	...	9 54
		dep	7 30	...	11 50	P.M.	1 5	7 49	...	...	...	9 55
*50¾	LISTOWEL	arr	**7 45**	...	**12 5**	...	1 20	**8 4**	...	...	...	10 6
		dep	**8 0**	...	**12 30**	4 30	1 25	**8 10**	...	...	...	10 10
57¼	LIXNAW	arr	8 13	..	12 44	4 44	1 39	8 25	...	. .	...	10 27
		dep	8 15	..	12 45	4 45	1 40	8 27	..	...	...	10 30
*62	ABBEYDORNEY ..	arr	8 28	...	1 0	4 54	1 49	8 39	...	...	...	10 39
		dep	8 30	...	1 2	4 55	1 50	8 42	...	...	...	10 40
65½	ARDFERT	arr	8 39	...	1 12	5 4	1 58	8 51	..	...	...	10 50
		dep	8 45	...	1 15	5 6	2 0	8 55	...	...	...	10 56
*70¼	TRALEE	arr	9 0	.	1 30	5 20	2 10	9 10	...	...	...	11 15
	Fenit Line.											
*70¼	TRALEE ...	dep	9 15	...	...	..	4 0	...	...	...	..	...
74¾	SPA	arr	9 25	...	...	...	4 10	...	...	...	...	...
		dep	9 26	...	...	...	4 11	...	...	...	...	...
76½	KILFENORA ...	arr	Flag.	...	...	..	Flag.	...	...	...	...	...
		dep		...	...	...		...	...	...	...	...
*78¼	FENIT	arr	9 35	..	...	...	4 20	...	...	...	...	...

Week Days.--No. 1—To pass No. 3 Down at Listowel.
No. 3—To pass No. 3 Down at Rathkeale and No. 6 Down at Listowel.
No. 5—To pass No. 6 Down at Abbeyfeale.
No. 6—To pass No. 7 Down at Newcastle and No. 9 Down at Listowel.

Stations marked thus (*) are Staff Stations
Bars across the Line thus (=) denote the places where trains cross or pass each other.
When descending the *inclines* at either side of *Barnagh Station*, Drivers and Guards are to see that sufficient brake power is applied, and when necessary by pinning down a number of Wagon Brakes to ensure perfect control of the Train.

A When required to shunt, attach or detach Vehicles at Barnagh, the work must be done on *the Siding*, and under no circumstances whatever on the Main Line.

Extract from the WL&WR Working Timetable of November 1895.

DOWN TRAINS—Fenit, Tralee and Foynes to Limerick.

Distance from Fenit	STATIONS		1 G.S. & W. Goods A.M.	2 G.S. & W. Pass. A.M.	3 Pass. A.M.	4 G.S. & W. Goods A.M.	5 G.S. & W. Pass. A.M.	6 Pass. Mail A.M./P.M.	7 Goods P.M.	8 P.M.	9 Mixed Mail P.M.	Sundays 1 Mixed Mail P.M.
	FENIT	dep	...	...	...	...	...	10 45	...	...	6 0	...
1¾	KILFENORA	arr	...	...	...	...	...	Flag.	...	...	Flag.	...
		dep	...	...	...	...	...		...	...		...
3½	SPA	arr	...	...	...	...	...	10 54	...	...	6 9	...
		dep	...	...	...	...	...	10 55	...	...	6 10	...
8	TRALEE	arr	...	...	...	...	...	11 5	...	...	6 20	...
8	TRALEE	dep	...	...	7 0	...	...	11 40	2 40	...	7 0	7 0
12¾	ARDFERT	arr	...	...	7 10	...	...	11 50	2 53	...	7 15	7 15
		dep	...	...	7 11	...	...	11 51	2 55	...	7 16	7 16
16¼	ABBEYDORNEY	arr	...	...	7 17	...	...	11 57	3 4	...	7 25	7 25
		dep	...	...	7 18	...	...	11 58	3 8	...	7 26	7 26
21	LIXNAW	arr	...	...	7 28	...	...	12 8	3 17	...	7 36	7 36
		dep	...	...	7 29	...	...	12 10	3 20	...	7 39	7 39
27½	LISTOWEL	arr	...	...	7 42	...	...	12 23	3 35	...	7 55	7 55
		dep	...	...	7 46	...	...	12 26	4 0	...	8 5	8 5
33	KILMORNA	arr	...	...	7 50	...	...	12 39	4 20	...	8 20	8 20
		dep	...	...	8 0	...	...	12 40	4 25	...	8 21	8 21
37	ABBEYFEALE	arr	...	...	8 8	...	...	12 48	4 35	...	8 30	8 30
		dep	...	...	8 10	...	...	12 50	4 45	...	8 31	8 31
40¼	DEVONROAD	arr	...	...	8 17	...	...	12 57	4 57	...	8 39	8 39
		dep	...	...	8 18	...	...	12 58	5 0	...	8 40	8 40
44¾	BARNAGH	arr	...	...	8 28	...	...	1 7	5 25	...	8 56	8 56
		dep	...	...	8 30	...	...	1 10	5 28	...	8 58	8 58
51	NEWCASTLEWEST	arr	...	...	8 45	...	...	1 25	5 50	...	9 13	9 13
		dep	...	...	8 55	...	...	1 35	6 53	...	9 23	9 23
53¾	ARDAGH	arr	...	...	9 2	...	...	1 40	7 3	...	9 29	9 29
		dep	...	...	9 3	...	...	1 41	7 8	...	9 30	9 30
59	RATHKEALE	arr	...	...	9 15	...	...	1 52	7 28	...	9 44	9 44
		dep	...	...	9 18	...	...	1 53	7 38	...	9 46	9 46
61	BALLINGRANE	arr	...	...	9 25	...	...	1 58	7 48	...	9 52	9 52
70½	FOYNES	dep	...	...	9 0	...	...	1 25	...	...	Mixed 5 30	...
64½	ASKEATON	arr	...	...	9 13	...	...	1 39	...	...	5 42	...
		dep	...	...	9 15	...	...	1 40	...	...	5 47	...
61	BALLINGRANE	arr	...	...	9 23	...	...	1 50	...	...	5 55	...
61	BALLINGRANE	dep	...	...	9 30	...	...	2 0	7 58 G.S & W.	...	9 53	9 53
67¼	ADARE	arr	...	...	9 43	...	...	2 13	8 13 Pass.	...	10 5	10 5
		dep	...	...	9 45	...	...	2 15	8 18 P.M.	...	10 7	10 7
71	PATRICKSWELL	arr	5 46	8 56	9 53	8 20	1 1	2 23	8 28	8 56	10 19	10 19
		dep	5 47	8 57	9 55	9 20	1 2	2 25	..	8 57	10 20	10 20
	FOYNES JUNCTION	pass	6	8 9	13	10 8	9 42	1 17	...	9 12	10 33	10 33
77½	LIMERICK CHECK	arr	...	...	10 10	...	...	2 45	8 55	...	10 35	10 35
		dep	...	...	10 12	...	...	2 47	8 58	...	10 38	10 38
78¼	LIMERICK	arr	6 9	9 16	10 15	9 45	1 20	2 50	9 0	9 15	10 40	10 40

Week Days.—No. 3—To pass No. 1 Up at Listowel and No. 3 Up at Rathkeale.
No. 6—To pass No. 3 Up at Listowel and No. 5 Up at Abbeyfeale.
No. 7—To pass No. 6 Up at Newcastle and No. 8 G.S. & W. Goods at Patrickswell.
No. 9—To pass No. 6 Up at Listowel.

When descending the *inclines* at either side of *Barnagh Station,* Drivers and Guards are to see that sufficient brake power is applied, and when necessary by pinning down a number of Wagon Brakes to ensure perfect control of the Train.

A When required to shunt or detach Vehicles at Barnagh, the work must be done on *the Siding,* and under no circumstances whatever on the Main Line.

Extract from the WL&WR Working Timetable of November 1895.

UP TRAINS. Limerick to

No. 1—To pass No. 1 Down at Athenry, No. 2 Down at Claremorris, No. 3 Down at Kiltimagh, and No. 5 Down at Swinford.
No. 2— ,, ,, No. 1 ,, ,, Ennis No. 2 ,, ,, Athenry, and No. 5 ,, ,, Claremorris.
No. 3— ,, ,, No. 2 ,, ,, Swinford.
No. 4— ,, ,, No. 2 ,, ,, Claremorris (precede No. 1 Up from Claremorris W. & L.) No. 5 Down at Tubbercurry.

Distance from Limerick.	STATIONS.	WEEK DAYS. 1 Mixed to Ennis Goods thence arr	1 dep	2 Mixed to Ennis Passenger thence arr	2 dep	3 Passenger arr	3 dep	4 Mixed arr	4 dep	5 Passenger arr	5 dep
		a.m.	a.m.	a.m.	a.m.	a.m.	a.m.	a.m.	a.m.	a.m	a.m
...	LIMERICK	...	2 30	...	6 45	...	...	...	...	...	...
¾	ENNIS JUNCTION ...	2 32	Pass.	6 47	Pass.	...	...	...	...	...	...
** 4	LONGPAVEMENT ...	2 39	2 40	6 56	6 57	..	...	...	...	...	...
9¾	CRATLOE	3 0	3 2	7 9	7 10	...	...	...	...	...	...
**13	SIXMILEBRIDGE... ...	3 12	3 15	7 18	7 23	...	...	...	...	...	...
16½	BALLYCAR	3 28	3 30	7 32	7 36		...	...	...	...	...
19¾	ARDSOLLUS	3 39	3 40	7 45	7 49		...	...	...		...
**23	CLARECASTLE	3 52	3 55	7 56	8 2		...	...	...		...
**24¾	ENNIS	4 0	4 30	**8 10**	**8 35**	Tuesdays and Saturdays	only.	...	...		...
**32½	CRUSHEEN	4 55	5 0	8 55	8 56		...	...	...	Wednesdays and Saturdays only.	...
36¾	TUBBER	5 10	5 13	9 6	9 7		.	...	...		...
**42¼	GORT	5 27	5 45	9 19	9 30		...	...	...		...
49	ARDRAHAN	6 2	6 8	9 45	9 50	...	...	...	...		...
**55	CRAUGHWELL	6 23	6 30	10 7	10 12	...	...	...	...		...
**60	ATHENRY	**6 45**	**7 5**	**10 30**	**11 15**	...	...	...	...	...	9 10
**69	BALLYGLUNIN	7 28	7 30	11 37	11 40	...	...	...	...	9 30	9 32
**76	TUAM	7 48	8 10	12 0	12 15	...	6 50	...	8 30	9 45 STOP	...
80¼	CASTLEGROVE	8 22	8 23	12 26	12 28	7 2	7 3	8 42	8 43	...	...
**84¾	MILLTOWN	8 33	8 38	12 39	12 40	7 13	7 14	8 52	8 54	...	...
**88½	BALLINDINE	8 48	8 52	12 50	12 51	7 24	7 25	9 4	9 6	...	...
**93	CLAREMORRIS W. & L.	**9 4**	**9 25**	**1 1**	**1 2**	7 35	pass	9 14	Pass	...	...
**93½	CLAREMORRIS Mid. ...	9 30	10 15	1 4	1 8	7 36	7 41	**9 16**	**9 35**	...	...
**102½	KILTIMAGH	**10 50**	**11 10**	1 30	1 35	8 6	8 8	10 0	10 2	...	...
**110½	SWINFORD	**11 30**	**11 55**	1 53	1 58	**8 27**	**8 31**	10 20	10 22	...	...
**117½	CHARLESTOWN	12 15	12 25	2 15	2 17	8 49	8 52	10 40	10 41	...	...
120	CURRY	12 35	12 40	2 24	2 26	9 2	9 3	10 51	10 52	...	...
**123¾	TUBBERCURRY	12 50	1 20	2 34	2 37	9 13	9 16	**11 0**	**11 14**	...	...
128¾	CARROWMORE	1 30	1 35	2 53	2 54	9 30	9 31	11 28	11 29	...	...
134	LEYNY	1 52	1 55	3 8	3 9	9 45	9 46	11 43	11 44	..	...
**138¼	COLLOONEY	2 7	2 30	3 19	3 24	9 56	10 0	11 55	12 4	...	...
**...	COLLOONEY East Cabin S.L.&N.Co.	...	...	...	...	...	...	...	...	...	...
**...	COLLOONEY North Cabin M.G.W.R.	2 32	...	...	3 26	...	10 3	...	12 6	...	..
**...	CARRIGNAGAT JN. ...	2 34	...	...	3 28	...	10 5	...	12 8	...	...
**...	BALLYSODARE ...	2 39	2 41	3 30	3 35	10 8	10 9	12 11	12 12	...	...
145½	SLIGO	2 52	...	3 45	...	10 20	...	12 25	...	...	...

Bars across the Line thus (=) denote the places where trains cross or pass each other.
Stations marked thus (**) are Electric Staff Stations.

Extract from the WL&WR Working Timetable of November 1895.

Ennis, Tuam, and Sligo.

6 Mail		7 Mixed from Ennis		8 Passenger		9 Passenger		1 Mixed to Ennis Goods		STATIONS
WEEK DAYS.								**Sundays.**		
arr	dep	arr	dep	arr	dep	arr	dep	arr	dep	
a.m.	a.m.	p.m.	p.m.	p.m	pm.	p.m.	p.m.	a.m.	a.m.	
...	10 40	...	3 20	...	...	...	7 10	...	2 30	LIMERICK
10 42	Pass	3 22	Pass.	...	...	7 12	Pass.	2 32	Pass.	ENNIS JUNCTION
10 50	10 51	3 30	3 31	...	...	7 19	7 20	2 39	2 40	LONGPAVEMENT
11 3	11 4	3 42	3 43	..	...	7 32	7 33	3 0	3 2	CRATLOE
11 11	11 12	3 50	3 51	...	...	7 40	7 41	3 12	3 15	SIXMILEBRIDGE
11 19	11 20	3 58	3 59	...	...	7 46	7 47	3 28	3 30	BALLYCAR
11 27	11 29	4 6	4 7	...		7 53	7 54	3 39	3 40	ARDSOLLUS
11 36	11 40	**4 14**	**4 16**	...	...	8 1	8 4	3 52	3 55	CLARECASTLE
11 45	11 55	4 20	4 45	...	...	8 10	...	4 0	...	ENNIS
12 15	**12 18**	5 5	5 7	..	...	STOP	...	...	...	CRUSHEEN
12 28	12 29	5 18	5 20	...	...	...		...	...	TUBBER
12 42	12 45	**5 33**	**5 45**	...	...		...	...	...	GORT
12 56	12 57	6 2	6 6	...	...			...	...	ARDRAHAN
1 11	1 14	6 21	6 27	...	...			...	...	CRAUGHWELL
1 30	**1 55** A	6 42	7 10	...	5 0			...	...	ATHENRY
2 17	**2 20**	7 30	7 33	5 20	5 23			...	...	BALLYGLUNIN
2 38	**3 0**	**7 50**	...	5 40	...			...	...	TUAM
3 10	3 11	STOP	...	STOP •--	...			...	...	CASTLEGROVE
3 19	**3 20**			...	...			...	. .	MILLTOWN
3 29	3 30			...	...			...	...	BALLINDINE
3 38	Pass			...	...			...	...	CLAREMORRIS W. & L.
3 40	**4 0**			...	...			...	...	CLAREMORRIS MID.
4 28	4 30			...	...			...	...	KILTIMAGH
4 49	4 52			...	...			...	...	SWINFORD
5 9	5 10			...	...			...	...	CHARLESTOWN
5 17	5 18			...	...			...	...	CURRY
5 28	5 4			...	...			...	...	TUBBERCURRY
5 46	5 47			...	...			...	...	CURRAMORE
6 0	6 1			...	...			...	...	LEYNEY
6 12	6 15			...	...			...	...	COLLOONEY
...	...			...	...			...	...	{ COLLOONEY East Cabin S.L. & N.C. { COLLOONEY North Cabin M.G.W.R.
...	6 17	...	...	...	...			...	...	
..	6 19	...	...	...	...			...	...	CARRIGANAT JUNCTION
6 22	6 23	...	...	...	...			...	...	BALLYSODARE
6 35	...	...	...	...	...			...	...	SLIGO

Column 7 vertical note: On Wednesdays and Saturdays this Train will not leave Athenry until 8.50 p.m.

Right margin note: No. 6—To pass No. 2 Down at Crusheen, No. 5 Down at Ballyglunin, No. 3 Down at Tuam, No. 6 Down at Milltown, and No. 5 down at Tubbercurry. No. 7—,, No. 5 Down at Clarecastle and No. 3 Down at Gort.

Bars across the Line thus (=) denote the places where trains cross or pass each other. Stations marked thus [**] are Electric Staff Stations.

Extract from the WL&WR Working Timetable of November 1895.

KILLALOE BRANCH

UP TRAINS.

Distance from Limerick.	STATIONS.		WEEK-DAYS 1 Psgr. A.M.	WEEK-DAYS 2 Mxd. P.M.	WEEK-DAYS 3 Psgr. P.M.	Sunday Passenger. P.M.
	LIMERICK ...	dep	10 55	3 25	7 25	...
¾	ENNIS JUNCTION	pass	10 57	3 27	7 27	...
4¼	KILLONAN ...	{ arr	11 5	3 35	7 34	...
		{ dep	11 6	3 37	7 35	...
8	LISNAGRY ...	{ arr	11 13	3 42	7 41	...
		{ dep	11 14	3 43	7 42	...
9¾	CASTLECONNELL	{ arr	11 19	3 49	7 48	...
		{ dep	11 21	3 52	7 49	...
*14½	BIRDHILL ...	{ arr	11 35	4 10	8 3	...
		{ dep	11 38	4 20	8 10	...
*17½	KILLALOE ...	arr	11 45	4 30	8 20	...

DOWN TRAINS.

Distance from Killaloe.	STATIONS.		WEEK-DAYS 1 Psgr. A.M.	WEEK-DAYS 2 Mxd. P.M.	WEEK-DAYS 3 Psgr. P.M.	Sundays Passenger. P.M.
	KILLALOE ...	dep	8 30	1 15	6 10	...
2¾	BIRDHILL ...	{ arr	8 37	1 23	6 16	...
		{ dep	8 40	1 30	6 20	...
7½	CASTLECONNELL	{ arr	8 51	1 43	6 31	...
		{ dep	8 52	1 45	6 32	...
9¼	LISNAGRY ...	{ arr	8 56	1 49	6 36	...
		{ dep	8 57	1 50	6 37	...
13	KILLONAN ...	{ arr	9 5	1 58	6 45	...
		{ dep	9 7	2 0	6 46	...
	ENNIS JUNCTION	arr	9 14	2 9	6 54	...
16¾	LIM'R'CK CHECK	{ arr	9 15	2 10	6 55	...
		{ dep	9 18	2 12	6 58	...
17½	LIMERICK ...	arr	9 20	2 15	7 0	...

Extract from the WL&WR Working Timetable of November 1895.

Chapter Eleven

The Line in the Twentieth Century

The absorption of the Waterford, Limerick and Western Railway into the Great Southern and Western system, while it did not result in the disappearance of the services it provided (which continue, much reduced so far as passenger trains are concerned, to the present day), did have some concomitant changes. In particular, the boat trains connecting with steamers from and to South Wales were diverted to another route. The GWR in England was by 1900 busy making arrangements for a packet service between Fishguard and Rosslare, so as to replace a 120 mile sea crossing by one half that length, and the GS&WR was simultaneously co-operating by developing a more direct route from Cork by way of Mallow, Dungarvan and Waterford to Rosslare, which only used the former WL&WR route to traverse Waterford. The chief *raison d'etre* of the line from Waterford to Limerick, to link the south-west of Ireland with Great Britain, was about to disappear. Entering from the east, the new line had a short stretch of joint GS&WR and Dublin & South Eastern Railway track between Abbey Junction and Joint line Junction. Beyond New Wharf and the grand new station was another new piece of line of half a mile, running to the west across the Suir viaduct and joining the Dungarvan line at Grace Dieu Junction. The first boat train in connection with the new route left Paddington for Fishguard on 30th August, 1906.

Bradshaw's Railway Guide of 1910, when these changes had been completed and the new pattern had settled down, shows what had happened. On the line between Waterford and Limerick the passenger services remained at five trains each way daily, which called at most or all intermediate stations. They did not terminate at Waterford but went through from or to Rosslare along the line through Wellington Bridge newly built by the GS&WR. They were ordinary trains with no special facilities. On the Cork-Mallow-Dungarvan-Waterford-Rosslare route, however, two corridor expresses ran each way daily; the stock was of bogie coaches newly built for the service, and new dining cars were also attached. The through journey took about four hours, with most stops being omitted. The crossing now took 3½ hours. To or from Fishguard from or to London sleeping berths were available for first class passengers, if one travelled by night. The WL&WR had never been able to offer anything as good as that from the Cork and Kerry areas, though Limerick passengers still used it, and those who lived along the route of the line. The new service by way of Rosslare did not, however, cause the withdrawal of the Waterford steamers, which still ran daily, making the night crossing, not now however to Milford but to Fishguard. For those not in a hurry who preferred to get a night's rest on board this was still a preferred option. This service was still operating in 1939, when the author used it both ways as a steerage passenger and had a comfortable night's rest in a third-class bunk.

Gradually the beautifully-liveried locomotives and coaches that Robinson had introduced were re-painted in the less-colourful livery of the GS&WR, black with red and white lining-out for the engines, dark chocolate brown for the coaches. Both locomotives and carriages from the GS&WR now began to infiltrate on to the

WL&WR system. Care had to be taken when marshalling former WL&WR stock with GS&WR vehicles, as the latter used a different kind of continuous brake which required two pipes instead of only one throughout the train in order to operate the wheel-brakes, so a second pipe had to be fitted to the coaches coming from the smaller company. The latter stock gradually became dispersed throughout the GS&WR system, as did its locomotives. Those built or designed by Robinson, efficient though they were, and with standard parts interchangeable with one another, were now odd-ones-out so far as the general stock of GS&WR engines were concerned, and most did not survive long for this reason. One retrograde step was the removal of electric lighting from some of the coaches which Robinson had designed and its replacement by gas; however, soon afterwards the GS&WR went over itself to electric lighting on the Stone system, with current generated by dynamos beneath the coach floors.

One may divide the 90-or-so years after the absorption of the WL&WR into its larger neighbour as having four periods: that of the still-independent GS&WR, that of the GSR, that of CIE and that of Iarnrod Eireann. The GS&WR years were reasonably prosperous until the coming of World War I, but Ireland felt the brunt of wartime conditions, more particularly by the inability to obtain coal (which had always been had from England, Wales or Scotland since it had few deposits of its own) and, later, first through political disagreement with Britain, then through its own Civil War, usually referred to as 'the Troubles', which added damage through sabotage to fuel shortage. As mentioned earlier, a Lancia armoured car of the Irish Free State Army was ambushed by the Republican Army at Farranalleen on the Thurles branch. After political settlement and the end of violence, the Irish Government, now independent of Great Britain, decided on a unified railway system to include all lines which were wholly within its own territory, and the subsequent amalgamation of 1st January, 1925 produced the Great Southern Railway. Reference to *Bradshaw* shortly before this shows that the former WL&WR route now had only four through trains daily, on schedules slower than in 1910, with no through trains on Sundays at all. By now it had become merely a branch of the larger system; the Works at Limerick were no longer in use for building engines.

During the next quarter-century the Great Southern system continued somewhat uncertainly to operate. Continually strapped for cash, it tried to save money by such methods as singling double-tracked routes, such as the main line of the former Midland Great Western between Dublin and Galway. The world-wide depression of the late 1920s and early 1930s hit the system hard, especially as road competition was now becoming a problem. Some lines were closed down, including many of the picturesque narrow-gauge railways in the west of Ireland. The Waterford to Limerick line did not have its services affected, at any rate before the outbreak of World War II; *Bradshaw* for 1938 shows a similar pattern of trains to 1922 - indeed, slightly better, with five westbound trains instead of four.

Between 1925 and 1929 the work of building the Ardnacrusha Power House brought extra traffic. This was connected by a 3 ft gauge railway of one mile to Longpavement Halt, which at one point crossed the Limerick-Ennis railway on the level. By 1930 this line was closed down, but a standard gauge branch was built in its place.

Swinford station on 23rd April, 1953, looking towards Sligo. *H.C. Casserley*

However, hardly was the railway system beginning to emerge from its earlier troubles when World War II broke out. Coal was once more unobtainable; Great Britain, now politically separated from its former possession, needed every ton it could produce; in addition, the insistence of the Irish Government in maintaining strict neutrality caused unfriendliness between the two Governments, so no generosity was to be expected. The consequence of the coal shortage was that many services had to be abandoned, or run only certain days during the week. Attempts were made to adapt locomotives to burn turf, but unsuccessfully. Once the war had ended the Irish Government, moved not by political principle but because it seemed in the interests of the whole community, took charge of public transport by road, rail or air, and formed a single company, Coras Iompair Eireann ('Irish Transport Company'); thus the Great Southern Railway became a part of CIE. There were further closures of lines to passengers, where motor coaches seemed the more convenient mode of travel. Steam gave place by degrees to diesel haulage; services generally improved in speed and comfort, and on-train catering improved with them, though as in Great Britain full restaurant service was largely replaced by buffet facilities. A final step, in 1987, was to separate the rail system from the road system, as Iarnrod Eireann. A final addition to the lines under survey was the Limerick Cement Factory Extension Railway. This opened on 1st October, 1957, from Rossbrien, near milepost 2 on the Kerry line, to the Castlemungret cement factory. The junction was operated with a key on the Patricks Well-Limerick Staff.

During the post-war years the service between Waterford and Limerick has continued to operate, though now the emphasis is on the carriage of bulk goods, such as cement, oil and (in season) sugar beet. The line itself is now entirely single, with passing facilities at Carrick-on-Suir, Clonmel, Tipperary and Limerick Junction. Manual signalling by semaphore and manual points-operation is still used. Passenger trains are now down to one a day in either direction, with an extra one during the summer. There is a proposal that the line should be worked by railcars - which would certainly be more economical than a diesel locomotive hauling no more than its own weight in coaches, as happens at present. It is much to be hoped that if this happens, and if sufficiently lightweight vehicles are used, the service could once more be extended from Limerick all the way to Sligo, since the rails are still *in situ* and carry freight.

Meanwhile the line is well, if not intensively used by freight services, with cement in bulk being moved from Waterford to Limerick, and bagged cement also being carried to Clonmel. Liner trains run both from Cork and Limerick to Waterford and vice versa in connection with cargo boats to and from Waterford. Trains with bagged fertiliser run from Limerick to Clonmel and Waterford, although the line from Waterford to New Ross closed to all traffic in the mid-1990s. Between September and December sugar beet trains run from their collection point at Wellington Bridge, on the Waterford-Rosslare line, to Mallow by way of Limerick Junction. Trains carrying the mails run at night between Waterford and Limerick. The line is certainly busy still, if not in the manner envisaged by Alexander Nimmo when he wrote his Report in the 1820s. There is no talk of its being closed.

The afternoon train from Limerick to Rosslare enters the main platform at Waterford on 10th July, 1992 behind diesel-electric Bo-Bo No. 146.   *Author*

Appendix One

Locomotives of the W&LR

Dimensions and details where known

Type	2-2-2	2-4-0	0-4-2	2-4-0	0-4-2	0-6-0	4-4-0	4-4-0	0-6-0	2-4-0	2-4-2T	0-4-2T	0-6-0	0-4-4T	0-4-4T	4-4-2T	4-4-0	0-4-4T
Maker	Stothert & Slaughter	Fairbairn & Sons	Sharp, Stewart & Co.	Vulcan Foundry	Avonside Engine Co.	Vulcan Foundry	Vulcan Foundry	Dübs & Co.	Dübs & Co.	Dübs & Co.	Vulcan Foundry	Limerick	Dübs & Co. (4) Kitson & Co. (4)	Limerick	Kitson & Co.	Kitson & Co.	Kitson & Co.	Limerick
Designer						H. Appleby	H. Appleby	H. Appleby	J.G. Robinson	J.G. Robinson	J.G. Robinson	J.G. Robinson	J.G. Robinson	J.G. Robinson	J.G. Robinson	J.G. Robinson	J.G. Robinson	J.G. Robinson
Date(s) obtained	1847	1853	1853-62	1874-82	1876	1883	1886	1886	1886	1889-94	1891	1892	1893-1900	1894	1895	1896	1896	1899
Number obtained	6	6	?	10	4	2	1	1	1	8	2	1	8	1	2	3	3	1
Cylinders (in.)	15 x 20	15 x 21	16 x 24	16 x 24	16 x 24	17½ x 26	17½ x 26	16½ x24	16½ x24	17 x 24	16 x 24	16 x 24	17 x 24	16 x 24	16 x 24	16 x 24	17 x 24	16 x 24
Driving wheels Diameter	5 ft 9 in.	5 ft 0 in.	4 ft 6 in.	5 ft 6 in.	5 ft 3 in.	5 ft 2 in.	5 ft 6 in.	5 ft 1 in.	4 ft 6 in.	6 ft 0 in.	5 ft 6 in.	4 ft 7 in.	5 ft 2 in.	4 ft 7 in.	5 ft 6 in.	5 ft 6 in.	6 ft 0 in.	5 ft 4 in.
Working pressure (psi)				150						160	150		150		150	150	150	150
Heating surface (sq. ft)				806	1,032*					991	806		991		780	780	887	808
Firebox heating surface (sq. ft)				88						107	88		107		88	88	107	88
Grate area (sq. ft)				15						17¾	15		17¾		15	15	17¾	15½
Loco. weight in working order					30 t.					36 t. 9 c.	45 t. 0 c.		36 t. 12 c.		43 t. 0 c.	46 t. 19 c.	40 t. 12 c.	49 t. 19 c.
Tender weight in working order					24¾ t.					22 t. 11 c.	-		27 t. 8 c.		-	-	27 t. 8 c.	-
Coal capacity										2½ t.	2 t.		4 t.		2 t.	1¾ t.	4 t.	2¼ t.
Water capacity (gallons)										2,000	1,200		2,000		1,200	1,040	2,000	1,200

*Note: * Heating surface including firebox.*

Appendix Two

Names and Numbers
of WL&WR Locomotives

Prior to 1886 most engines had numbers only, but by 1897 nearly all the locomotives of the Waterford, Limerick and Western Railway had received names; even the goods engines enjoyed titles, often suggesting a giant capacity for work. Names were taken from Irish legend, history or prominent features of the landscape. *Galtee More*, *Knockma*, *Nephin* and *Slieve na Mon* were all mountains, whilst *Sir James* Spaight, the *Earl of Bessborough* and Percy *Bernard* were the names of Chairmen or Board members. The names of homes of Directors were bestowed on numbers 13, 15, 16, 51 and 54. The older class 2-4-0s carried the names of flowers and some 0-6-0s those of insects. *Geraldine* is a notable dynasty, *Garryowen* an alternative for Limerick whilst *Sarsfield* recalls the victor at the local battle here in 1690. Fifty years since the incorporation of the W&LR were celebrated by No. 53 *Jubilee*. After the line was absorbed into the GS&WR, a company which named very few of its engines, WL&WR locomotives had their nameplates removed when they were renumbered and re-liveried on passing through the shops at Inchicore and Limerick. The following is a complete list of the locomotives acquired by the GS&WR on 1st January, 1901.

WLW No.	GSW No.	Type	Builder's No.	Built	Wdn	Name	Comment
1	221	0-6-0ST	RS 2379	1884	1909		Rebuilt 1899 from 0-6-0.
2	222	0-6-0	Kit 3908	1899	1949	Shannon	GSR class 'J25'.
3	260	0-4-2T	Kit 1783	1872	1912	Zetland	Rebuilt 1892 from 0-4-2.
4	(223)	0-6-0	SS 1345	1862	1901		Rebuilt from 0-4-2.
5	224	0-6-0	SS 1346	1862	1909	Bee	Rebuilt 1893 from 0-4-2.
6	225	0-6-0	SS 1529	1864	1907	Ant	Rebuilt 1890 from 0-4-2.
7	226	0-6-0	Kit 1784	1872	1905	Progress	Rebuilt 1888 from 0-4-2, renamed *Wasp* in 1893.
8	(261)	2-4-0	VF 910	1881	1902	Primrose	
9	262	4-4-0	Dübs 2194	1886	1912	Garryowen	
10	263	2-4-0	Dübs 2477	1889	1907	Sir James	
11	(264)	2-4-0	Fbn	1853	1903		
12	265	2-4-0	VF 1162	1886	1907	Earl of Bessborough	Rebuilt 1894 from 4-4-0.
13	266	2-4-2T	VF 1315	1891	1934	Derry Castle	GSR class 'F5', sold in 1914 to Cork & Macroom Direct Railway and became GSR No. 491 in 1925.
14	267	2-4-2T	VF 1316	1891	1935	Lough Derg	GSR class 'F5'.
15	268	0-4-4T	SS 740	1859	1914	Roxborough	Rebuilt 1894 from 0-4-2.
16	269	4-4-2T	Kit 3616	1896	1957	Rocklands	GSR class 'C5'.
17	270	4-4-2T	Kit 3617	1896	1949	Faugh a Ballagh	GSR class 'F5'.
18	271	4-4-2T	Kit 3689	1897	1949	Geraldine	GSR class 'F5'.
19	(272)	0-4-2	AE 1126	1876	1901	Kincora	
20	273	2-4-0	Dübs 2880	1892	1909	Galtee More	
21	274	4-4-2T	Kit 3690	1897	1949	Blarney Castle	GSR class 'F5'.
22	275	2-4-0	Dübs 2662	1890	1913	Era	
23	276	2-4-0	Dübs 2881	1892	1949	Slieve na Mon	GSR class 'G3'.
24	227	0-6-0	Dübs 2195	1886	1910	Sarsfield	
25	(277)	2-4-0	VF 706	1874	1902	Verbena	Formerly *Limerick*.
26	278	0-4-2	AE 1125	1876	1910		

WLW No.	GSW No.	Type	Builder's No.	Built	Wdn	Name	Comment
27	279	0-4-4T	AE 1127	1876	1953	Thomond	Rebuilt 1899 from 0-4-2, GSR class 'E1'.
28	(280)	2-2-2	Kit 1213	1864	1902	South of Ireland	
29	228	0-4-0ST	SS 1653	1865	1925		
30	281	2-4-0	VF 707	1874	1903	Lily	Formerly Waterford.
31	282	2-4-0	VF 708	1874	1910	Myrtle	Formerly Ennis.
32	283	2-4-0	VF 709	1874	1910	Dahlia	Formerly Tuam.
33	(284)	0-4-2	AE 1128	1876	1901		
34	(229)	0-6-0T	AE 1243	1878	1901		
35	285	2-4-0	VF 911	1881	1911	?	Formerly Duncannon.
36	286	2-4-0	VF 913	1881	1904	Violet	
37	287	2-4-0	VF 912	1881	1909	Camelia	
38	288	2-4-0	VF 990	1882	1907	Hyacinth	
39	289	2-4-0	VF 991	1882	1905	Shamrock	Formerly North Star.
40	230	0-6-0	VF 1010	1883	1909	Vulcan	
41	231	0-6-0	VF 1011	1883	1910	Titan	
42	(232)	0-6-0WT	H(L) 284	1862	1901		Purchased 1886.
43	290	2-4-0	Dübs 3025	1893	1951	Knockma	GSR class 'G3'.
44	291	2-4-0	Dübs 3026	1893	1959	Nephin	GSR class 'G3'.
45	233	0-6-0	Dübs 3042	1893	1919	Colleen Bawn	
46	234	0-6-0	Dübs 3043	1893	1911	Erin-go-Bragh	
47	292	2-4-0	Dübs 3109	1894	1915	Carrick Castle	
48	293	2-4-0	Dübs 3110	1894	1954	Granston	GSR class 'G3'.
49	235	0-6-0	Dübs 3222	1895	1928	Dreadnought	GSR class 'J22'.
50	236	0-6-0	Dübs 3223	1895	1951	Hercules	GSR class 'J22'.
51	294	0-4-4T	Kit 3587	1895	1910	Castle Hacket	
52	295	0-4-4T	Kit 3588	1895	1954	Brian Boru	GSR class 'E2'.
53	296	4-4-0	Kit 3618	1896	1949	Jubilee	GSR class 'D15'.
54	297	4-4-0	Kit 3619	1896	1928	Killemnee	GSR class 'D15'.
55	298	4-4-0	Kit 3694	1897	1949	Bernard	GSR class 'D15'.
56	237	0-6-0	Kit 3691	1897	1951	Thunderer	GSR class 'J22'.
57	238	0-6-0	Kit 3692	1897	1934	Cyclops	GSR class 'J22'.
58	239	0-6-0	Kit 3693	1897	1949	Goliath	GSR class 'J22'.

Two further locomotives were built for the WL&WR, but delivered new in 1901 to the MGWR:

4	-	0-6-0	Kit 3974	1900	1929	Shamrock	Became MGWR 141, GSR 233.
11	-	0-6-0	Kit 3975	1900	1929	Samson	Became MGWR 142, GSR 234.

Abbreviations

AE	Avonside Engine Co., Bristol.
Dübs	Henry Dübs & Co., Glasgow.
Fbn	William Fairbairn & Son, Manchester.
H(L)	Hawthorns & Co., Leith.
Kit	Kitson & Co., Leeds.
RS	Robert Stephenson & Co., Newcastle.
SS	Sharp, Stewart & Co., Manchester.
VF	Vulcan Foundry, Newton-le-Willows.

Note

GSW numbers in parenthesis were allotted but not actually carried, due to early withdrawal.

Appendix Three

Capital and Revenue Accounts of the W&L&WR for the Year ending 30th June, 1899

Capital Account

CAPITAL: Authorised stock and shares: £1,603,530; loans: £949,031; Government grant: £150,000. Total: £2,702,561. The subjoined statement of stock and share capital created shows the proportion received to 30th June, 1899.

Description	Created £	Received £
Ordinary £50 shares	598,600	597,550
Ordinary £12½ shares	512 ½	
4% Consolidated preference	713,645	670,235 ¾
5½% Preference £25 shares (Foynes Amalgam. 1873 Act)	26,025	26,025
5% Preference £25 shares (Ennis Amalgam. 1873 Act)	8,395	7,550
3½% Perpetual preferential stock	328,267	299,799 ¾
TOTAL	1,675,374 ½	1,601,160

RECEIPTS & EXPENDITURE The receipts and expenditure on capital account to 30th June 1899 were as under:

Received	£	Expended	£
Shares and stock	1,601,160	Lines open for traffic	2,137,988
Debenture stock	932,364	Working stock	327,244
Forfeited shares gain, less discount on issuing shares, &c.	10,555	Subscriptions other railways	115,895
Government grant	150,000		
Baronial shares	120,000	Collooney & Claremorris	279,115
Premium on baronial shares	7,356		
Debit balance	38,806		
TOTAL	2,860,242		2,860,242

The estimate of further expenditure required: £2,238 for the half year ended 31st December, 1899. The assets to meet this amounted to *nil.*

Revenue Account

The receipts and expenditure on this account for the half-years ended 30th June and 31st December, 1898 are shown in the subjoined statement:

	1898 *31st Dec.* £	*1899* *30th June* £
Coaching traffic	45,936	45,045
Goods, minerals & cattle	57,570	55,282
	103,506	100,277
Special & Miscellaneous	2,189	2,065
Gross receipts	105,695	102,342
Expenditure	64,025	60,402
Net	41,670	41,940
Add sundry balances & interest, &c.		
(net)	3,337	3,322
Total net revenue	45,007	45,262
Deduct: Interest, preference dividend, &c.	43,842	43,994
Balance to next accounts	1,165	1,268

(From *Bradshaw's Shareholders' Guide*, 1900: p. 307.)

A good investment for the shareholders. 0-4-0 saddle tank No. 29 about to shunt a train out of the platform at Limerick at 3rd September, 1900. Built in 1865, this locomotive worked for 60 years, most of them on pilot duties at Limerick.

LCGB/Ken Nunn Collection

Appendix Four

The Cahir Accident, 1955

No accidents or incidents occurred on the lines the WL&WR owned or managed during its years of independence which involved a passenger being killed, except that in June 1874 at Tipperary station a ticket collector tried to prevent a man from boarding a moving train; in the scuffle that followed both fell from the platform under the wheels of the moving vehicles and were killed. Some did occur in which company servants lost their lives, as on 21st August, 1875 when, as a goods train from Ennis was approaching the bridge over the Shannon into Limerick, one of the locomotive's tyres snapped and caused it to leave the rails and plunge down the side of the embankment; the driver was seriously injured and the fireman was killed. Perhaps the most remarkable happening during these years was when an engine which had been detached from its train in Ennis station on 10th June, 1876 moved off on its own, the driver being elsewhere and the fireman, though on the footplate, not noticing what was happening until the locomotive was well under way! After it had proceeded for a mile he managed to reverse it and bring it back, but struck the standing train violently, damaging a van and two carriages.

The most serious and spectacular accident on what had been the company's main line occurred long afterwards, in the days of CIE ownership, at Cahir in the early morning of 21st December, 1955. A train loaded with sugar beet was on its way from Bridgetown, in County Wexford, to the beet factory at Thurles, travelling by way of Waterford and Limerick Junction. The locomotive was No. 375, one of the 2-6-0 Moguls designed by R.E.L. Maunsell at Ashford on the SE&CR and built at Woolwich Arsenal, being subsequently sold to the MGWR and assembled by them. They were well liked by the men who drove and fired them once the knack had been discovered of how to handle them, but they seem to have had an Achilles heel, insufficient braking power. They used both steam and vacuum braking and their counterparts in England, which had to descend very severe gradients on the Barnstaple-Ilfracombe line, had been fitted with additional brake cylinders. The train on this occasion was 32 wagons and a guard's van, weighing together with engine and tender some 560 tons. There were no brakes on the wagons, so that control could only be exercised on the locomotive and tender and, to a small extent, from the guard's van.

The train was late leaving Waterford and suffered further delay at Clonmel, and did not approach Cahir station until 4.30 pm. Meanwhile, at Cahir, the night mail bound eastward had drawn into the platform on the south side and was taking water. Its rear end fouled the points of the loop, so the distant and home signals were set to stop the beet train before it entered the station. But the latter's locomotive was apparently out of control. It whistled to give warning but did not stop. Observers on the platform saw sparks flying from the wheels of No. 375, which showed that the brakes were being applied. It passed into the loop and continued on to the short siding which extended out towards the bridge over the Suir, burst through the buffer stop and went on to the bridge itself, which had, of course, no rails beyond the buffers but only planking and the bridge's lower cross-girders. These could not support the weight of the locomotive, which fell through on to the river bank, followed by the heavy tender and several beet-filled wagons. The driver and fireman were killed immediately by the tender crushing them on the footplate.

When the locomotive was examined afterwards it was found that the valve gear had been put into reverse and that the regulator was fully opened; evidently the driver had tried this final desperate measure to bring the train to a halt. What could not be established at the subsequent inquiry was whether the engine's brakes had failed or whether they had been applied too late in the course of the descent to Cahir, which includes 2 miles at 1 in 150. The Inspecting Officer, in the Official Report issued four months later, found that the accident had occurred because the train was out of control when it approached and passed through Cahir station, and that he could offer no explanation except that the driver failed to keep it under control and obey the signals. Action to stop the train had been left until it was too late.

The footplatemen on the locomotive at the head of the night mail, which was standing in the station at the time, were sure that when they saw the two men on the footplate of No. 375 as it passed them, they looked 'just the same as if nothing was going to happen.' The impression left on the reader, imaginatively re-creating the accident in his mind, is one of perplexity, with the abiding image of the two men going calmly to their deaths and accepting it with resignation. Their names are commemorated on a memorial tablet set up in Cahir station, paid for by subscriptions from CIE staff.

The aftermath of the accident at Cahir in December 1955. The 2-6-0 and its tender beneath the broken flooring of the bridge over the River Suir.   *Irish Railway Record Society*

Bibliography

Locomotive and Train Working in the Latter Part of the 19th Century, Vol. 6, E.L. Ahrons, Heffers of Cambridge, 1954.

Bradshaw's Shareholders' Guide, Volumes from 1848 to 1901.

Robinson Locomotives, B. Haresnape & P. Rowledge, Ian Allan, 1982.

150 Years of Irish Railways, F. Mulligan, Appletree Press, Belfast, 1983.

The Great Southern & Western Railway, K.A. Murray & D.B. McNeill, Irish Railway Record Society, 1976.

Irish Steam, O.S. Nock, David & Charles, 1982.

J.G. Robinson, A Lifetime's Work, David Jackson, Oakwood Press, 1996.

Outline of Irish Railway History, H.C. Casserley, David & Charles, 1974.

Regional History of Railways Vol. 16, J.W.P. Rowledge, Atlantic Transport Publishers, 1995.

Journal of the Irish Railway Record Society: various issues.

Railway Magazine: various issues.

Irish Ordnance Survey Maps: ½ in. to 1 mile: Nos. 17, 18, 22, 23.

Acts of Parliament

Geo. IV, cap. 139, 31st May, 1826.
Victoria, cap. 131, 21st July, 1845.
Victoria, cap. 231, 22nd July, 1847.

A view from the train looking along the platform at Cahir towards Waterford on 12th April, 1955.   *R.M. Casserley*